GU00468249

Focus
on the
Bible

Focus
on the
Bible

H.J. Richards

Dedication

In memory of
Fr Robert Dyson, SJ
(1895-1959)
who
for all his strange ways
gave his students
an abiding love of the Bible.

First published in Great Britain in 1989 by
KEVIN MAYHEW LTD
Rattlesden, Bury St Edmunds
Suffolk IP30 0SZ

ISBN 0 86209 100 4

© 1989 H.J. Richards and Kevin Mayhew Ltd

All scripture texts are taken from *The New Jerusalem Bible*, published
and copyright 1985 by Darton, Longman and Todd Ltd and Doubleday
& Co Inc, and are used by permission of the publishers.

We gratefully acknowledge the use of copyright photographs throughout
this book.

Cover photograph © Carlos Reyes/Andes Press Agency, of 'Adam and
Eve', from a tapestry in Turvey Abbey, Bedfordshire
Cover design by Rob Williams
Typesetting by David Holland Graphics, Colchester, Essex
Printed by J.B. Offset (Marks Tey) Ltd., Marks Tey, Essex

Contents

Introduction

© Andes Press Agency

It is Sunday morning, and you've gone as usual to the 9.30 at your parish church. As always, after the introductory prayers, you stand up with the rest of the congregation to 'greet the Gospel'. The Bible is solemnly carried in procession, escorted by candles, and greeted with alleluias. When the procession reaches the lectern, the priest or deacon may even honour the book with incense, in the way kings have always been honoured in some countries. The reading from the Bible is announced. Everyone says, 'Glory to you, Lord', and when it is finished, 'Praise to you, Lord Jesus Christ'. It is as if Christ has been present in the reading, and spoken in person. The kiss which the reader gives to the book is a mark of respect and affection which is not even given to the Eucharist. Clearly what the whole ceremony emphasises is the sacredness of the Bible. The whole Bible. It is one book, and all of it is the Word of God.

It is Tuesday evening, and you've gone as usual to the parish Bible discussion group. The same Bible is open on the table, round which many members of the Sunday congregation are sitting in a much more informal atmosphere. You have come to try to understand the Bible more deeply. The points that are raised, and the questions that are asked, continue to be respectful, but also quite critical. In this setting, the Bible is no longer simply a single divine voice. It is quite explicitly a piece of human literature – in fact five or six dozen pieces – and you are analysing them as you would any other pieces of literature. What is emphasised tonight is no longer the heavenliness of the Bible, but its earthliness.

Do these two weekly experiences contradict each other? If you are sincere about one, can you be serious about the other? Is the tension between the Sunday and the Tuesday eventually going to give you a headache, or perhaps even turn you into a split personality?

This book has been written to assure Christians that they need have no such fears. The Bible is not *either* the Word of God *or* the words of men – it is both. We do not have to be *either* believers *or* scholars – we can be both. We do not have to be afraid that emphasising the human aspect of the Bible – and there will be plenty of that in this book – will make it less the Word of God. God's activity does not exclude human activity. In fact, God's most distinctive way of acting is in and through human beings. And the Bible is the supreme example of that.

© Andes Press Agency

The Bible: *A Human Book*

Human Voices

It is no bad thing to begin a study of the Bible by sampling a few of the things actually to be found there, rather than the kind of things we might expect. They will indicate, more clearly than anything else, what kind of book we are dealing with. For example, how would you judge this piece?

> I shall bring my work to an end here. If it is well composed and to the point, that is just what I wanted. If it is worthless and mediocre, that is all I could manage.
>
> *(2 Maccabees 15:37-38)*

Hardly the voice of someone conscious of divine inspiration. The author seems almost flippant. But then the New Testament can make off-the-cuff remarks in much the same way:

> I am thankful that I did not baptise any of you, except Crispus and Gaius, so that no one can say you were baptised in my name. (O yes, I did baptise the family of Stephanas too; but besides these I do not think I baptised anyone).
>
> *(1 Corinthians 1:14-16)*

> When you come, bring the cloak I left with Carpus in Troas. And the scrolls. Especially the parchment ones.
>
> *(2 Timothy 4:13)*

Does one need divine guidance to make worldly-wise observations such as the following?

> Whoever at dawn loudly blesses his neighbour –
> it will be reckoned to him as a curse.
> The dripping of a gutter on a rainy day
> and a quarrelsome woman are alike;
> whoever can restrain her, can restrain the wind,
> and take a firm hold on grease.
>
> *(Proverbs 27:14-16)*

Is divine guidance even thinkable in the following piece? Who would today give this advice to parents?

> Whoever loves his son will beat him frequently
> so that in after years the son may be his comfort . . .
> Pamper your child and he will terrorise you,
> play along with him and he will bring you to sorrow.

> Do not laugh with him, or one day you will weep with
> him
> and end up gnashing your teeth . . .
> Bend his neck in youth,
> bruise his ribs while he is a child,
> or else he will grow stubborn and disobedient,
> and hurt you very deeply.
>
> *(Ecclesiasticus 30:1-12)*

Here is Luke's comment on how writing an 'inspired' Gospel did not absolve him from having to do a good deal of laborious research:

> Seeing that many others have undertaken to draw up accounts of the events that have reached their fulfilment among us, as they were handed down to us by those who from the outset were eyewitnesses and ministers of the word, I in my turn, after carefully going over the whole story from the beginning, have decided to write an ordered account for you.
>
> *(Luke 1:1-3)*

© Barnaby's Picture Library

9

Here is how Paul writes to the Christians of Salonika:

We want you to be quite certain, brothers, about those who have fallen asleep (in death), to make sure that you do not grieve for them, as others do who have no hope. We believe that Jesus died and rose again, and that in the same way God will bring with him those who have fallen asleep in Jesus. We can tell you this from the Lord's own teaching, that we who are still alive for the Lord's coming will not have any advantage over those who have fallen asleep. At the signal given by the voice of the Archangel and the trumpet of God, the Lord himself will come down from heaven; those who have died in Christ will be the first to rise, and only after that shall we who remain alive be taken up in the clouds together with them to meet the Lord in the air.

(1 Thessalonians 4:13-17)

Paul twice assumes that Christ's 'coming' is to take place in his own lifetime, and assumes it so naturally that many of his readers actually gave up their jobs. Had he overdone it? He must have thought so, because a few months later he had second thoughts (after all, he was only human), and wrote again:

About the coming of our Lord Jesus Christ, brothers, and our being gathered to him: please do not too easily be thrown into confusion or alarmed by . . . any statement or any letter claiming to come from us suggesting that the Day of the Lord has already arrived.

(2 Thessalonians 2:1-2)

How human Jeremiah can be is revealed in an excerpt from his private diary:

A curse on the day when I was born!
May the day my mother bore me be unblessed!
A curse on the man who brought my father the news,
'A son, a boy has been born to you!'
May this man be like the towns
that Yahweh overthrew without mercy . . .
for not killing me in the womb;
my mother would have been my grave
and her womb pregnant for ever.
Why did I ever come out of the womb
to see toil and sorrow
and end my days in shame?

(Jeremiah 20:14-18)

There is no mistaking the utterly human tone of words like these. Or indeed of all the words quoted above, limited as they are, and hesitant, provisional, groping, banal, even flippant. Because they have been bound into the covers of a book we call the Holy Bible, we tend to read them with *a priori* assumptions in our mind. But no one coming across them for the first time would conclude, *a posteriori*, that such words are divine, or inspired, or absolute, or anything other than the fallible words of fallible human beings. How horrified Paul would have been if he thought that people would seize on the letters he had written to the young churches he founded – even the postcard he wrote to Philemon – and place them alongside the Psalms and Prophets as 'Holy Scripture'.

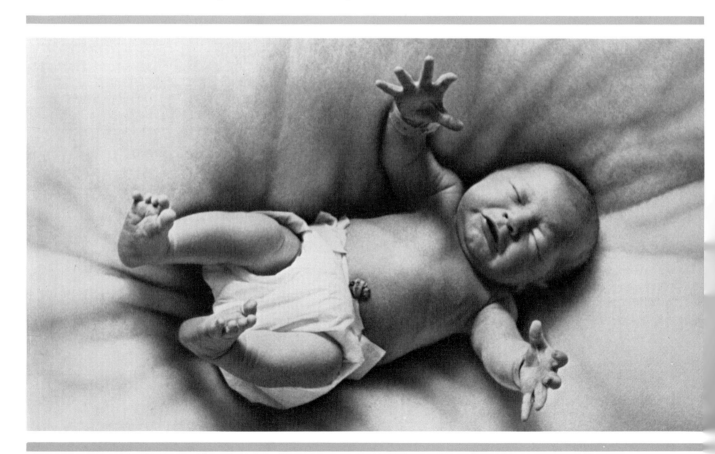

Human Variety

To drive the point home, a few more quotations. Pick up your Bible and leaf your way through. What sort of things do you find? Let's take a look.

In the beginning God created heaven and earth. Now the earth was a formless void, there was darkness over the deep, with a divine wind sweeping over the waters.

If one of the animals that you use as food dies, anyone who touches the carcase will be unclean until evening; anyone who eats any of the carcase must wash his clothing and will remain unclean until evening.

Yahweh, God of my salvation,
when I cry out to you in the night,
may my prayer reach your presence,
hear my prayer for help.

How beautiful are your feet in their sandals,
O prince's daughter!
The curve of your thighs is like the curve of a necklace,
work of a master hand.

After this, Jesus went with his disciples into the Judaean countryside and stayed with them there and baptised. John also was baptising at Aenon near Salim, where there was plenty of water.

Then the angel showed me the river of life, rising from the throne of God and of the Lamb and flowing crystal-clear. Down the middle of the city street, on either bank of the river were the trees of life.

The quotations are taken more or less at random, from the beginning, the middle, and the end of the Bible. Because all of them are set out in the same print, and written in the same kind of English, we tend to read all of them in the same tone of voice.

Would we do so if the different parts of the Bible had been written in a quite different English, and if each part had been set out in a different style, and if each part had been bound separately to make a collection of seventy or so different books?

The Bible is a whole shelf-full of books. History books, pieces of legislation, essays, diaries, story books, prayers, visions, itineraries, family trees, songs, hymns, love poems, letters, sermons, theological articles – a whole shelf-full of books.

For various reasons we have put the whole shelf between two covers. But that shouldn't make us forget the rich variety of literature contained within these two covers, each with its own tone of voice. You don't read a letter from your lawyer in the same tone of voice as a letter from your fiancée. You don't read a piece of theology the same way as a gas bill.

We might say, 'Yes, but even so we do acknowledge this collection of books as the one Word of God.' Indeed we do, and this will be the subject of the next section. But we can say, 'Word of God, Word of God' till we're blue in the face. If we don't take into account the human form in which that Word comes to us, we'll simply misunderstand it. If we don't first of all see it as five or six dozen different pieces of human literature, we won't be able to hear what God may be trying to say to us through them.

The different tones of voice in which we have to read the Bible are known as *literary forms*. Literary forms are like the key signature written at the head of each piece of music. The music will only sound like what the composer had in mind if you play it in that key. Misread the key, and you'll get discord. There's no point in playing a piece in the 'key' of history if the author had some entirely other 'key' in mind. Least of all if you are doing so out of respect for the author. It would be the grossest disrespect.

Unfortunately these key signatures are not printed out at the head of each piece in the Bible. But then they're not printed out in our newspapers either, yet we normally distinguish one piece from another without any great difficulty. We don't read the short story in the same 'key' as the editorial. We switch into the right 'key' automatically because we recognise immediately what the writer is up to.

We don't so easily recognise the dozens of literary forms used by the biblical writers, especially if they are forms no longer used in modern literature. We need the advice of experts, even if they don't always agree. We need to tread warily.

Human Errors

Die Bibel Hat Doch Recht was the bold title of a book by the German scholar Werner Keller – *The Bible Was Right After All!* Beautifully produced, with hundreds of excellent illustrations, it set out to prove that detail after biblical detail, which many critics had said could not possibly be true, *were* true.

The book became very popular, and one can understand why. For a hundred years and more, beginning with Charles Darwin, the Bible had had such a battering from the scientists that many ordinary folk were beginning to think that it had been totally discredited. The stories were all make-believe, fiction, fairy tales, hardly worth the paper they were printed on. Yet here was photo after photo to prove the opposite. The archaeologists had dug up ruins and monuments and inscriptions to put the record straight.

For example, where the book of Exodus said that the Egyptian Pharaoh had press-ganged the Hebrews into slavery, there was a painting of Semitic slaves working for the Egyptians.

Where the book of Kings said that king Hezekiah built a tunnel to divert the Jerusalem water-supply, there was a tunnel brought to light again by the spade.

Where the Acts of the Apostles said that so-and-so was governor of such-and-such a town, there was an inscription with his name on it.

It was natural that the more conservative should seize on this kind of archaeological evidence. The spade had proved that the Bible was true after all.

The trouble is, of course, that archaeology works both ways. Certainly there are many things in the Bible which it can back up, and Keller's photos do it very well. But there are other cases (which Keller doesn't say too much about) where archaeology proves the Bible wrong even where no one suspected it of being wrong.

For instance, the book of Exodus says that the name Moses means 'Rescued out of the water'. The archaeologists have produced dozens of examples where it obviously means nothing more than 'Son'. Three of the Pharaohs mentioned in ancient Egyptian monuments are called Tuthmosis (son of Toth), Ramesses (son of Ra), and Ahmosis (son of the god Ah).

Or again, take the list of the forefathers of the human race listed in the book of Genesis:

Adam lived for 800 years after the birth of Seth and he fathered sons and daughters.
In all, Adam lived for 930 years; then he died.
When Seth was 105 years old he fathered Enosh.
After the birth of Enosh, Seth lived for 807 years, and he fathered sons and daughters.
In all, Seth lived for 912 years; then he died.
(and so on)

Two things need to be said about these phenomenal ages. Firstly they are far too high to be real – archaeology can show that no member of the human race ever hit such a high score. But secondly they are far too low to do what they're supposed to do, which is to add up to the total age of mankind. Archaeology can show that mankind is much older than these lists suggest. The first man appeared on earth millenia before 4004BC.

Another example. The Bible lists a number of towns that Israel is said to have conquered at the end of the exodus from Egypt. Archaeologists have dug up these old towns. Some of them didn't even exist when the Israelites first came into Palestine from the desert. Someone's made a mistake.

In short, the evidence of archaeology can work both ways. It can prove the Bible accurate on all sorts of points where people said it was inaccurate. But it can also prove the Bible inaccurate on all sorts of points where people presumed it was accurate. Archaeology raises as many questions as it answers.

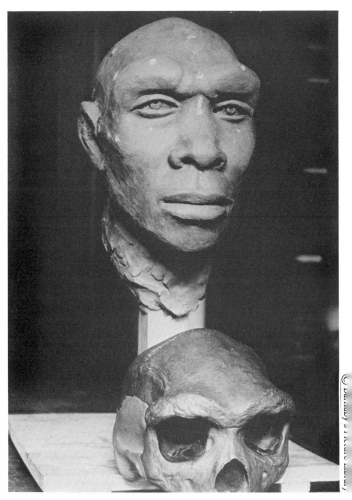

Skull of Aurignacian Man, about 25,000BC.

This means that if we ask, 'Is the Bible true?', there's little point in going to the archaeologists for an answer. Perhaps we would do better to ask, 'What sort of truth are we looking for in the Bible?' If it's the truth about history, or geography, or biology, or any other science, then we should go to the experts. That is their field, after all. The people who wrote the Bible were not concerned with questions of that sort, and could make errors there as easily as any other human authors. They simply used what science they had, or geography, or history – and it was pretty primitive, as everyone else's was until quite recently – to answer questions of a much deeper sort.

They weren't concerned with the How or the When or the Where of the human race. They were concerned with the deeper questions – Who and Why.

They didn't write to inform people about the meaning of Moses's name, but about the meaning of Moses's life. They didn't write to tell us how old our forefathers were before they died, but how they are related to each other and to God. They didn't write to instruct their readers about how many towns they must overcome to bring about the Kingdom of God, but about how many times they must overcome themselves.

And given the importance of that, perhaps we can forgive them the errors they made in the far less important matters which didn't really concern them. As Galileo said, 'The Scriptures weren't given to us to show us how the heavens go, but how to go to heaven.'

Human Story-telling

On a holiday I once spent in the east, I was talking to a Greek monk (in very broken Greek) about the great split between the eastern and western Church which took place over a thousand years ago. I asked him what he thought about this matter. To answer me, he took a piece of paper and tore it in half. One half he put carefully into his breast pocket, next to his heart, saying, 'The Eastern Church'. The other half, called 'The Western Church', he tore in half, and in half again, then in half three more times. Then he threw the thirty two scraps in the air. We were climbing mount Sinai, and the sight of those bits of confetti eddying around the crags, some dropping but others wafted higher and higher by the wind, has remained with me much longer than anything he might have said.

When I reflected on the incident, I realised how typically eastern that monk had been. We in the west, when we want to make a point, do it most typically in a speech or an article, explaining our argument as clearly and logically as we can. The easterner, most typically, puts his point into action, and lets the action speak for him. The westerner, when pushed, becomes more and more abstract. The easterner, when pushed, becomes more and more concrete.

We often forget – or think it makes no difference – that the Bible comes to us from the east. It is *about* people from the east, and was *written* by people from the east, and was originally designed to be *read* by people from the east. So the stories it tells are not (usually) of people explaining things, but of people doing things – Adam and Eve, Cain and Abel, Noah and the Ark, Abraham, Isaac and Jacob, Moses and Pharaoh, Kings and Prophets.

Even the New Testament, right down to what they call the most theological piece in it (the Gospel of John), is full of the things Jesus *did* – at Cana in Galilee, at the well in Samaria, in the starving desert, down at the blind man's pool, over in Bethany at Lazarus's tomb, on the lake in Peter's boat.

In fact, even when Jesus speaks instead of doing things, and people are expecting him at last to give them all the answers, what does he do? He tells them stories of people *doing* things – the Good Samaritan, the Pharisee and the Publican, the Prodigal Son, the Shepherd and his Sheep, the Wise and Foolish Bridesmaids. All very eastern. And unless we orientate ourselves to this mentality (which means literally 'to go eastern'), we shall misunderstand the Bible.

The Bible is made up of stories. The stories are not told to entertain us, or even to inform us, but only to make a point in a dramatic and concrete way. Unless that point comes across to us, the story has been a waste of time.

We westerners tend to be rather dismissive of stories – 'That is *only* a story' – forgetting the power of stories not only to stick (look how my Greek monk has stuck, not only with me but now with you as well!), but to mould our lives and give us all the values we live by. Yet they remain stories, not reports or accounts to be scientifically analysed.

If I had stopped my Greek monk in the middle of his act, and started counting those pieces of paper, or measuring them, or comparing one piece with another – he might just as well have thrown *me* down the mountain! That wasn't the point of his act. His act had a meaning, and it was the meaning he wanted me to see.

Or again, if you had stopped me while I was telling that story, demanding to know precisely when I claimed it had taken place, or on what part of the mountain, or even whether it had taken place at all (because I *could* have made the whole thing up) – you would have missed the point. I didn't tell the story to inform you about what happened on my holiday, but to make a point.

The Bible doesn't tell us its stories because certain things happened, but because stories make a point. Adam and Eve, the Exodus, the Feeding of the Thousands, the Raising of Lazarus – these are not news bulletins. They are stories with a meaning. That's the eastern way of writing. Biblical orientation means getting on to that human wavelength.

I don't mean they're just tall stories. But I *do* mean they are deep stories, and they are true not because they happened, but because they're deep. The story of the Good Samaritan isn't proved true when you can point to the actual spot where it all took place. It is true when you can see the deep meaning of it for yourself.

Human Repetition

One of the very puzzling features in the Bible is that every so often you come across the same story twice.

We don't find it so odd when this happens in two different books. Mark tells us a story about Jesus, and we're not surprised to find that Matthew tells it too, and Luke as well for good measure. They're each writing their version of the Good News about Jesus. And presumably they each thought the story was too good an illustration to leave out.

But when the same story occurs twice in the same book, what then? One of the most well-known examples is the story of Jesus using just a few loaves to provide a meal for thousands of people in the desert. If you look at Mark you'll see that although he's got the story in chapter 6, he repeats it all over again in chapter 8, with only the slightest variations about the number of loaves, and the number of leftovers, and the number of people. All the rest is the same.

MARK CHAPTER 6	MARK CHAPTER 8
34 He saw a large crowd; and he took pity on them . . .	1 A great crowd had gathered . . .
36 'Send them away to buy themselves something to eat' . . .	2 'I feel sorry for all these people . . .
38 He asked, 'How many loaves have you? . . . They said, 'Five' . . .	3 If I send them off home hungry they will collapse on the way' . . .
39 Then he ordered them to get all the people to sit down . . . and they sat down on the ground . . .	5 He asked them, 'How many loaves have you?' And they said to him, 'Seven.'
41 Then he took the five loaves . . . and said the blessing; then he broke the loaves and began handing them to his disciples to distribute among the people . . .	6 Then he instructed the crowd to sit down on the ground, and he took the seven loaves, and after giving thanks he broke them and began handing them to his disciples to distribute . . . among the crowd.
42 They all ate as much as they wanted. They collected twelve basketfulls of scraps of bread . . .	8 They ate as much as they wanted, and they collected seven basketfulls of the scraps left over.
44 Those who had eaten the loaves numbered five thousand men.	9 Now there had been about four thousand people.

© UNRWA

'They all ate as much as they wanted.'

Matthew copied these texts of Mark almost word for word. Because it happened twice? That's unlikely – in the second story the disciples are just as surprised as in the first. They don't react as if they'd seen it all before. In fact, when Luke came to write up the story, with Mark's text in front of him, he only put in one version, not two. So did John.

This telling of the same story twice happens much more often in the Old Testament. There's a famous – and unedifying? – story of Abraham passing off his beautiful wife Sarah as his sister, so that the king of Egypt (who fancies her) will treat him well. Lo and behold, eight chapters further on, the same thing happens to Abraham all over again, with the king of the Philistines. And six chapters later it's happening again in Philistine country, only this time to Isaac and his wife Rebekah. Were these patriarchs always at it? Or is it the same story in three different versions?

Then there's the well-known story of creation. Everyone knows the opening chapter of the Bible where, over succeeding days, the original chaos slowly becomes an ordered world, so that on the sixth day man and woman can be brought on stage as king and queen of all they survey. Yet in the following chapter the creation starts all over again, with man as the first creature on stage, and all the animals (including woman!) last. Why is the story told twice, with those variations?

Or take the famous story of the rise to power of Israel's first king, Saul. In one version, Saul is God's choice, and God has to explain this carefully to an unknown prophet named Samuel, so that he's ready to arrange the coronation. But there's another version of the story, now interwoven with the first, where Saul is the unknown figure, and the already well-known prophet Samuel tells the people quite roundly that to choose a leader other than himself is an act of rebellion against God. Which version is factual?

When we reflect on examples of this kind, we realise again how difficult it is to answer the question, 'Is the Bible true?' True in what sense? True in telling us exactly what went on, and where, and when, and how? No. The Bible often contradicts itself. It hasn't got just one version of what really happened, but often two or more. It doesn't pretend to be an extended newsreel, covering the years 4000BC down to Christ.

If we can accept that, then perhaps we are ready to go deeper. The stories are not told because that's exactly how things took place. The stories are told because they illustrate, each in its own way, something about the human race's relationship with God. It's that relationship with God they invite us to explore, whether the story is told once, twice, or more times.

Summary

If you were God, how would you speak to the world? Perhaps by divine dictation, through a human mouthpiece if necessary, and a single one to ensure consistency. Presumably you would speak in the same tone of voice throughout, so that there would be no confusion.

Presumably what you said would be without any errors, guaranteed accurate and reliable. Presumably you would speak in a way that was immediately accessible to all cultures and mentalities, not in a way that was limited to only one. And presumably you would speak without repetitions, especially variant ones, lest your audience or readership should be left in doubt.

All this is precisely what the Bible has not got.

The one thing you would certainly *not* do is to speak your divine message through fifty different authors, of varying ability; or in a hundred different literary forms, with no indication of which is which; or in material that is in no way guaranteed free of factual errors; or in a style which is so eastern that we westerners have difficulty in tuning in. The one thing you would not do is to say your piece through stories, which are so open-ended that people can take from them what they wish. Least of all in stories that sometimes duplicate and contradict each other.

All this is precisely what the Bible has got. That is how thoroughly human it is.

How on earth can something that is as thoroughly human as that be regarded as the Word of God? This we must now consider.

Things to do . . .

You are going to be shipwrecked on a desert island. Which eight books of the Bible will members of your group take with them? Why? If all these books are the Word of God, what entitles people to be so choosy?

Your group is put in charge of a Time Capsule for future generations to find. There is room for sixty or seventy pieces of writing (history, poetry, letters, official documents, etc.) that will sum up the characteristics of the British people. No dates will be attached, or any indication of the kind of literature these writings are. Which pieces will you choose? Compare your choice, if possible, with that of some other group. Consider the implications for the sixty or seventy pieces of writing in the Bible.

Pinter's plays are separated from Shakespeare's by 400 years. The earliest writings of the Bible (1100BC) are separated from the latest (AD100) by three times as long, and from us by eight times as long.
Do you need help to understand Pinter and Shakespeare?
Do you need help to understand the Bible?

The Bible: *The Word of God*

There are two things I find absolutely essential for life:
without them this wretched existence would be
intolerable.
As long as I am locked up in the prison of my body,
I confess I need two things: light and food.

And so, Lord, you have given me
your sacred Body to nourish my body and mind,
and your Word to light the way for my feet.
Without these two, I could not live the good life,
for the Word of God is the light of my soul,
and your Sacrament is the bread that gives me life.

I would even call these the two tables
that furnish the two sides of the Church's treasure-
house.
One is the table of the sacred altar
on which lies the holy bread, the precious Body of
Christ.
The other is the table of the Law of God,
which teaches us the true faith and safely leads us
beyond the veil into the Holy of Holies.
(The Imitation of Christ, IV,11,ii. Author's
translation)

How Does God Speak?

Thomas a Kempis' fine words are well known. He regards the Bible with the same veneration as the Eucharist. For him, probably much more strongly than for us, both were essential for life. Without one, he would starve. Without the other, he would lose his way.

Was he being naïve? Do we have the same confidence as he did in calling the Bible the 'Word of God'? Would we use the term more hesitantly and with more reservation? Especially in the light of the thoroughly human characteristics we have analysed above?

Put it this way. To say, 'The Bible is the Word of God' is the same as saying, 'Here God *speaks* to us.' Now, there is no particular difficulty about accepting that God really is speaking when we read such words as:

Be still and know that I am God (Psalm 46)

or

Thou shalt love the Lord thy God with thy whole heart and thy whole mind (Deuteronomy 6)

or

Be ye compassionate as your heavenly Father is
(Luke 6)

or

He who has seen me (Jesus) has seen the Father
(John 14)

and so on.

But how are we supposed to understand that God is speaking to us when, for example, the words are addressed to God himself?

Out of the depths I cry to thee O Lord (Psalm 130)

Or worse, when the text tells me to do something I wouldn't dream of doing?

Spare the rod and spoil the child (Proverbs 13)

Or worse still, when the text begins to inveigh *against* God?

How long, Yahweh, will you remain hidden? For ever?
Is your anger to go on smouldering like a fire?
Remember me; how long have I left?
For what pointless end did you create all the children
of Adam?
(Psalm 89)

How can this be God speaking to *me*?

© Barnaby's Picture Library

Worst of all, what am I to make of texts which approve of actions which today we recognise as plainly immoral?

Samuel said to Saul . . . 'This is what Yahweh Sabaoth
says . . . "Go and crush Amalek; put him under the
curse of destruction with all that he possesses. Do not
spare him, but kill man and woman, babe and
suckling, ox and sheep, camel and donkey." ' . . .
Saul then crushed the Amalekites . . . He took
Agag king of the Amalekites alive and, executing the
curse of destruction, put all the people to the sword.
But Saul and the army spared Agag with the best of the
sheep and cattle the fatlings and lambs and all that was
good. They did not want to consign these to the curse
of destruction; they consigned only what was poor
and worthless.
The word of Yahweh came to Samuel, 'I regret
having made Saul king, since he has broken his
allegiance to me and not carried out my orders.'
Samuel was appalled and cried to Yahweh all night
long.
In the morning, Samuel set off to find Saul . . . He

said, 'Why did you not obey Yahweh's voice? . . . Is Yahweh pleased by burnt offerings and sacrifices, or by obedience to Yahweh's voice?' . . .

Samuel then said, 'Bring me Agag king of the Amalekites!' Agag came towards him . . . Samuel said: 'As your sword has left women childless, so will your mother be left childless among women!'

Samuel then butchered Agag before Yahweh at Gilgal.

(1 Samuel 15)

What is God supposed to be telling me in a text like that? How on earth can this be the Word of God?

Metaphor

How would one begin to answer questions as difficult as this? Perhaps, first of all, by recognising that when we call the Bible the 'Word of God', we are using a metaphor. God has not literally got words that he speaks, or a voice, or a mouth, or a larynx. Yet he does communicate himself. He does reveal himself. He does show himself. To say that the Bible is God's 'Word' is a metaphor to express the fact that in its pages God lets us know something about him. But metaphors must not be taken literally, or pressed too hard.

Nor must we turn this metaphor into something exclusive. To call the Bible the 'Word of God' doesn't mean that nothing else can be the Word of God – it obviously can, and more needs to be said about this later. Or again, to call the Bible the 'Word of God' doesn't mean it isn't the words of men – it clearly is, as the analysis above has presumably shown.

Perhaps the point can be made by referring to a delightful *Barnabas* cartoon. Adam and Eve are holding hands in the Garden of Eden. Adam says, 'It's lovely here, Eve. Just the two of us.' An angry voice booms from the sky, 'Just *how many* of us did you say, Adam?' An embarrassed Adam apologises: 'Sorry, Lord. Just the *three* of us, I meant to say.' He adds under his breath, 'I never was very good at mathematics.'

As an example of humour, perhaps we can award Barnabas an A plus. As an example of theology, C minus. Because God is not someone who can be added to Adam and Eve to make three. God is not a being alongside other beings. He is the ground in which all beings are rooted.

This means that God and man do not exclude each other in the way that one human being and another human being exclude each other. To say that Richards wrote this book means that Edwards didn't. But you couldn't say the same thing about God. God is not related to human beings in the way human beings are related to each other. If a human being does something, it does not mean that God is idle. If God does something, it does not mean that the human being is idle.

So the Bible may remain totally human, and still be called the 'Word of God'. The emphasis on the human input into the Bible does not mean that God's input is less. God does not act *instead* of man, filling in what men can't do. God's most characteristic activity is in and through the flesh of human beings. That is what the word *incarnation* ('in the

flesh') means. On this too, more will be said below.

So we return again to the question. If the Bible remains a thoroughly human book, what can it possibly mean to call it (even metaphorically) the Word of God?

What It Can't Mean

We have seen what it can't mean. It can't mean, for instance, that its words were *dictated* to the authors of the various books. The text simply doesn't bear out such a suggestion. The authors speak like themselves, and each is distinct from all the others. They haven't been 'taken over' by God in that way.

Nor can it mean that the various books contain *no errors*. There are numerous errors in the Bible – historical, geographical, scientific – as we have seen. It is not an infallible mine of information on all subjects under the sun. It is as fallible as any other human writing. It has to be, if we are to be serious about it being written by human beings.

Nor can it mean that there is anything *absolute* about the Bible. The biblical absolutist would like to be able to stick a pin into any page, and imagine that what the text says is what God is saying to him. For two pins he might find himself landed with the texts of Matthew 27 and Luke 10: 'He went away and hanged himself', 'Go thou and do likewise'. Clearly, the Bible must not be made into an absolute. Only God is absolute. However devoutly we wish to treat it as the Word of God, we must recognise its relative nature. The crib in Bethlehem was not the best of all possible cribs. The conditions in the Nazareth home were not the best of all possible conditions. And the words of the Bible are not the best of all possible words. The Bible is not the Word of God full stop. The Word of God comes to us *relativised*, and we must come to terms with that.

What It Does Mean

This chapter has been rather negative. We have spent a lot of time explaining what it *can't* mean to call the Bible the Word of God. It is time to be more positive. What *does* it mean?

It means that the Word of God, God's revelation of himself to the human race, can't be perceived direct, only through the thoroughly human form in which it is addressed to us. God speaks to us, not through a divine loudspeaker out of heaven, but in the voices and thoughts and ideas of our fellow human beings. Our God is not to be found in the extraordinary, the odd, the unusual, but in the usual, the normal, the ordinary. God's Word, like his presence, is an *incarnate* one. He speaks, like all important people, not directly, but 'through sources close to him'.

There are those who would prefer a Word of God that was dis-incarnate. A clear voice out of the sky would be less ambiguous, more direct. For them, the kind of Word here being described is too oblique, too problematical, too challenging. It no longer solves problems for me, or saves me the bother of thinking. I can no longer ask Moses, or David, or Hosea, or Matthew, or Paul, or even Jesus to tell me the answers to my questions. Instead, I have to ask, 'If

Moses, or David, or Hosea, or Matthew, or Paul, or even Jesus, thinking as they did in the world they lived in, saw their relationship to God in those terms – in what terms must I see it, thinking as I do in the world I live in?' And answering such questions is going to make heavy demands on me. Revelation is no longer contained in Scripture as in a carrier bag into which I can dip. Revelation is reflected in the Bible, through the eyes of its writers.

But when that revelation reflects into me, when what God spoke to Moses or David or the rest gets on to my wavelength, then indeed God speaks through these people to me.

It may worry some people that God's Word comes to us in such a roundabout way. But they ought to take consolation from it. After all, is not this how God has always spoken to the human race, and still does so? It's not only in the Bible that God's voice can be heard, but in all the events of our lives. It's not only by Jews and Christians that God's Word can be heard, but by people who have never even come across a Bible. St John puts it in these words:

In the beginning was the Word . . .
Its life was the light of men . . .
giving light to everyone . . .
(and the) power to become children of God.
(John 1:1-12)

Jesus puts it even more colourfully:

Imagine a sower going out to sow . . .
Some seeds fell into rich soil,
grew tall and strong,
and produced a good crop;
the yield was thirty, sixty, even a hundredfold . . .
What the sower is sowing is the Word.
(Mark 4:3-14)

God's Word has always produced a crop, because he has never stopped broadcasting it.

Why the Bible?

But then, if God speaks to all people in all the events of their lives, why the Bible for heaven's sake? Why accord it such a privileged position?

As regards the New Testament, the answer is obvious enough. This is the record of how the first generation of disciples saw and understood and interpreted Jesus. As such, it is irreplaceable. We will always have to refer back to this collection of writings if we want to test our own understanding of Jesus. These writings tell us, in a way nothing else can, what the impact of Jesus was, and why people thought that God 'spoke' through his life.

But why the Old Testament? Surely that has become redundant for Christians? Can it possibly have anything relevant to say to followers of Jesus?

Of course it can – in fact it must. Why? Precisely because what we call the Old Testament was *his* Bible. This was where he first found God. These writings were for him the Word of God: can they be regarded as anything less by his followers? Indeed, his followers must understand them as he did, as a Jew does. Unless they do this, they will never really understand Jesus.

Those who follow Jesus can't afford to neglect the Old Testament. By accepting Jesus, they have become part of Jesus' people, and committed themselves to that people's Bible. The Old Testament is the story of the pilgrimage of faith of the people we belong to. This is where our family have given witness to their faith, and recorded what they have seen and heard of God. And although that can never become simply a substitute for our own faith – which by definition has to be our own – we still need the richness of their thinking to feed us and challenge us, and above all to rebuke our own thinking, with all its superficiality, its narrowness, its inadequacy, its self-centredness, and its destructiveness. It is through the witness of these writings, as we reflect upon them over and over again, that God continues to speak to us. Without this witness, we wouldn't know who we are.

There is yet a further reason for Christians to approach the Old Testament with love and reverence. They go there not only to discover Jesus' God, but (in some way) to discover Jesus himself. Why on earth should Christians find Jesus in the Old Testament? Very simply, because they acknowledge him as the Word of God, the embodiment in a human being of the same Word that had been spoken throughout Israel's history. So Christians find nothing artificial in hearing overtones of Jesus' life and death in the stories of Adam, or of the Exodus, or of the Temple, or of the Exile and Restoration. It was in those events that God's Word had come to the Jewish people. That same Word became flesh in the person of Jesus of Nazareth. In him the whole story of the Old Testament is summed up and fulfilled. It is as if God were saying 'Look *this* is what I've been trying to tell you all along.'

The Word Made Flesh

Perhaps we could sum up this chapter by exploiting this parallel that Christians have made between the Bible and Jesus, calling them both the Word of God.

We will misunderstand Jesus if we take shortcuts. It is a shortcut to say that he was a man, full stop. This simply saves the bother of trying to cope with the deep mystery contained within this man. But it is just as much a shortcut to say he was God, full stop. This also simply saves the bother of coping with the fact that he was, unlike God but like each one of us, totally rooted in one limited part of history.

Some people try to solve the problem by cutting Jesus in two, half God and half man. For some of the things he did, like growing and suffering and dying, he was operating as it were on his human engine. But for other things, like healing people and multiplying food and rising from the dead, he switched over to his divine engine. But that is a shortcut too. Jesus lived one life, with one heart and soul, not two.

In order to remain true to the tradition that has been held from the beginning, what the Christian has to say is not that Jesus was a man in a sense which would exclude God, nor that he was God in a sense which would exclude man, nor that he was half of one and half of the other like a mermaid or a centaur. The Christian has to say that he was fully human, and fully divine. He was the whole truth about God lived out in the life of an ordinary human being. He was the Word of God.

We have to say the same kind of thing about the Bible if we are going to call that too the 'Word of God'. It is not simply human full stop, a piece of human literature exactly like any other. Nor is it simply divine full stop, a newscast sent out from heaven in a foreign language. Nor can we say that some parts of it (the nice bits) are divine, and the nasty bits human. To be true to Christian tradition, we've got to say it is the whole truth about God expressed in ordinary human terms. It is totally human from beginning to end. But in the same breath it is totally divine.

It is difficult to keep the correct balance on this. We tip the balance most easily when we so emphasise the divine aspect of the Bible that we think we can open it anywhere, point to a text, and say, 'That's what God is telling me to do.' He's not. That may have been what God was telling David, or Isaiah, or Paul. But in the light of that, we've got to make up our own mind what he's telling us to do.

But if that is the case, why call it the 'Word of God'? Because here is a record of the way in which our people, the family we belong to, have found God, and heard his voice, and understood what he asks of them and what he calls them to. All of it is expressed in utterly human terms, and therefore inadequately. But if God is going to make himself known to the human race, how else can he be understood except in human terms, however inadequate they are? Yet through these human terms, it *is* God who is expressed. It remains the Word of God.

Obviously this does not absolve us from doing any thinking for ourselves. We can't say, 'That's how people understood God then, so that's how I shall understand God now.' On the contrary, as has now been pointed out several times, what we have to say is, 'If that is how people saw God and his demands in their age, with their understanding of the world, how must I see his demands in this age, with my twentieth century understanding of the world?'

God certainly continues to speak to us through the Bible. But that doesn't mean that the Bible is a heavenly tape-recording instructing me what to do. At the end of our Bible readings in church we say, 'This is the Word of the Lord.' Perhaps we ought to say, 'Listen for the Word of the Lord.' What is he saying to me through this reading? Perhaps something different from the text? He speaks to us in the interaction between the Bible and the listener.

We musn't make the Bible into a God. Only God is God.

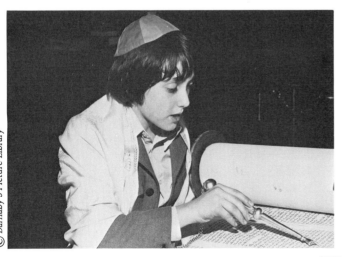

© Barnaby's Picture Library

Things to do . . .

Each member of the group chooses a passage of Scripture (Old Testament or New), and tries to put it as accurately as possible into its context. Then ask, how did the writer see God's demands in that context? If you put this passage into today's context, do the demands change? In the group, compare your choices, and your conclusions.

The Old Testament

*B*ible is a Greek word meaning 'book'. Of all books, Christians regard it as the most outstanding. For them, it is *The* Book.

Since it was written by many hands, it could accurately be described as a collection of sixty or seventy different books. But since Christians hear the one God speaking to them throughout the whole collection, they rightly regard it as one book, and bind it within two covers as a single work.

The one Bible nevertheless falls into two distinct parts, known as the Old Testament and the New Testament. *Testament* means a covenant, or agreement, or contract, by which two parties bind themselves to each other.

The Old Testament is the story of the solemn contract which the people of Israel believe God made with them through Moses. It consists of forty or so books.

The New Testament is the story of the solemn contract which Christians believe God made with them through Jesus. It consists of twenty seven books.

This section deals with the books of the Old Testament.

If you look at the Contents page of your Bible, you will probably find that it sets out the books of the Old Testament in four groups: Legal Books, Historical Books, Doctrinal Books, and Prophetical Books. This grouping has become common since the thirteenth century, when it was thought logical to divide the books up under these headings.

The Jews divided their Bible quite differently into three, reflecting the order in which the three groups of books were formed. They called these three groups The Law, The Prophets, and The Writings.

Since the heading under which we place a book influences the way we read it, it would be useful to respect the original headings given to these books by the Jews. For them, the Old Testament consists of:-

A. The Law

At the heart of this group stands the law by which Moses believed that God wanted his people to live. It is introduced by an explanation of the events necessary for understanding this law, and is completed by the later developments of the law of Moses.

Genesis
Exodus
Leviticus
Numbers
Deuteronomy

B. The Prophets

This group has collected together the preaching of the prophets, and prefaced it with their interpretation of the events through which they lived.

Joshua	Hosea
Judges	Joel
1 Samuel	Amos
2 Samuel	Obadiah
1 Kings	Jonah
2 Kings	Micah
	Nahum
Isaiah	Habakkuk
Jeremiah	Zephaniah
Ezekiel	Haggai
	Zechariah
	Malachi

C. The Writings

This group contains the miscellaneous liturgical, philosophical and narrative writings which were the last to be formed into a collection.

	Deutero-canonical
Psalms	
Proverbs	Baruch
Job	Judith
Song of Songs	Tobit
Ruth	Ecclesiasticus
Lamentations	Wisdom
Ecclesiastes	1 Maccabees
Esther	2 Maccabees
Daniel	
Ezra	
Nehemiah	
1 Chronicles	
2 Chronicles	

The Old Testament Books in Context

The Old Testament covers a period of at least two thousand years, from Israel's patriarchal ancestors down to New Testament times. The books of the Bible which cover this enormous period of time cannot be fully appreciated unless they are placed in the context not only of the events on which they comment, but of the date when the books were written. The table which follows provides a rough guide to these contexts, and may be found useful for reference.

Books of the Bible	History of Israel	Contemporary Events	Date
			BC
Genesis 12-50	Patriarchs immigrate into Palestine	Middle East invaded by Amorites	2000
		Egyptian rule in Palestine.	
	Emigration to Egypt.	Hyksos kings in Egypt.	1500
	Slavery in Egypt.		
Narratives of	Escape from Egypt under Moses.	Egypt vs. Hittites in	1300
Exodus & Numbers	Mount Sinai.	Palestine.	
Joshua	Occupation of Palestine.	End of Hittite power.	
Judges	Struggle for independence, especially against Philistines.	Philistines invade Palestine.	1200
1 Samuel	Saul anointed king.	End of Egyptian power.	1100
2 Samuel	King David.	End of Philistine power.	1000
Some Psalms	Israel's Golden Age.	Assyrian Empire established.	
Genesis 2-11	First writing of patriarchal traditions.		
1 Kings	Solomon.		
	Schism of Kingdom into north (Israel) and south (Judah).		
2 Kings	Elijah and Elisha.	Assyria extends Empire south.	900
			800
Amos			
Hosea	Israel crushed by Assyria and exiled.	Rome founded.	
Isaiah 1-39, Micah	Judah threatened		700
Jeremiah			
Deuteronomy	Religious reform in Judah.	End of Assyrian Empire.	600
Nahum	Deuteronomic History (Joshua-Judges-Samuel-Kings).		
Zephaniah	Judah exiled to Babylonia.	Babylon rules Middle East.	
Ezekiel			
Isaiah 40-55			
Habakkuk	Discussion of problem of evil.		
Proverbs, Job			
Leviticus	Codification of Law.		
Laws of Exodus and Numbers	Priests assume leadership.		
Genesis 1			
Haggai	Return of exiles to Jerusalem.	Persia rules Middle East.	
Zechariah 1-8			
Some Psalms	Building of second Temple.		
	Break with Samaria.	Roman Republic established.	500
Ezra-Nehemiah	Jerusalem rebuilt.	Golden Age of Greece.	
Chronicles			
Malachi, Joel	Reform movements.		400
Obadiah			
Isaiah 56-66			
Ruth, Jonah		Persia defeated by Alexander. Greek Empire.	
Zechariah 9-14	End of Prophetical Movement.	Rise of Roman Power.	300
		Roman Wars with Carthage.	
Tobit, Ecclesiasticus	Greek influence.		200
Ecclesiastes			
Song of Songs			
Daniel	Maccabee revolt.		
1 & 2 Maccabees	Jewish independence.	End of Greek Empire.	
Judith, Esther			
Wisdom		Rome rules the world.	
	Dead Sea Scrolls	Gallic Wars.	100
	Herod the Great.	Pompey and Caesar.	
		Augustus, first Emperor.	

Those whose eyes mist over before an array of dates even as simplified as the ones above, may be helped (as I was in the early stages of my studies) by at least knowing the magic word AMDEX, whose initials stand for the great turning points in Old Testament history – Abraham, Moses, David, Exile, Xt. They fall roughly (but only very roughly) into periods of 500 years.

Abraham	2000BC
Moses	1500
David	1000
Exile	500
Xt	0

Proto- and Deutero-Canonical

Canon means 'rule'. The canon of the Bible is the list of books which believers accept as ruling their lives. They return to them constantly in order to measure their faith and practice against them. Books included in the list are called *canonical*. Those excluded are called *non-canonical*.

The Jews of Jesus' time did not agree about the canon of their Bible. Those who lived in Palestine accepted a list of thirty eight books, which became known as the first or *proto*-canon. The Jews living in the Greek world outside Palestine accepted a longer list which included seven more recently written books – Baruch, Judith, Tobit, Ecclesiasticus, Wisdom, 1 Maccabees, 2 Maccabees. These books are known as *deutero* (second)-canonical.

The Christian Church was born in Palestine, but grew to adult age among the Greek-speaking Jewish communities outside Palestine. It was inevitable that Christians should adopt the longer canon of those communities, though disputes continued for centuries about whether the extra seven books had the same authority as the others. The Protestant reformers eventually omitted them from their Bible, referring to them as the *Apocrypha*. Interestingly, the Church of England still requires them to be printed as an appendix to the English Old Testament, and to be read 'for example of life and instruction of manners.'

A. The Law

The Law of the Lord is perfect,
refreshment to the soul . . .
The commandment of the Lord is pure,
light for the eyes.

(Psalm 19:7-8)

The Law you have uttered is more precious to me
than all the wealth in the world.

(Psalm 119:72)

How I love your Law!
I ponder it all day long.

(Psalm 119:97)

These quotations make it clear that for Jews the word 'law' does not have the negative overtones it tends to have for us – of rules and regulations, restraint and enforcement. For Jews, their Law is not a burden but a joy. In fact, 'law' is not really the right translation of the name the Jews give to this part of their Bible. The Hebrew word *Torah* means something more like 'teaching' or 'guide for living'. Its books contain quite as many stories as pieces of legislation. All of it, stories as much as laws, is a guide for living, and is gratefully received.

To appreciate this to the full, go and take part in a Jewish Sabbath service. The handwritten *Torah* scroll is kept in the most prominent part of the synagogue, in a sort of central 'tabernacle', with a lamp always burning before it. During the service, it is brought out and carried round the congregation, with worshippers leaning out of their seats to touch it, before it is placed on the desk for the readings. It is treated like the living presence of God among his people, in a way no mere 'code of laws' could ever be treated.

1. The Books of the Law

Although the *Torah*, in the form in which we now read it, was conceived of as a single work, it has been subdivided for convenience into five books. In fact the Greeks called it the *Pentateuch* (meaning 'five volumes'), and we still know the five books by their Greek titles – Genesis, Exodus, Leviticus, Numbers, Deuteronomy. The Jews have always known them (as Catholics know papal encyclicals) by the opening words of each book.

Genesis

Genesis means 'Beginnings'. Through its stories of the beginnings of the world, of the human race and of Israel, it sets out to teach the fundamental truths about man's relationship with God. God is he who created all that exists, and who has spoken to us to tell us of himself and to enter into a solemn pact or covenant with us.

This decisive entry of God into our history begins with **Abraham** (more about Abraham on page 24). The traditional stories which are told from chapter 12 onwards have preserved the essential belief that God called him out of his pagan background and established him in the land of Palestine. Through Abraham's complete giving of himself to God – which is what the word faith means – the process whereby sin came into the world was reversed, and all nations saw the beginning of their salvation.

The chapters which precede these stories are only there to provide the context needed to understand what God is believed to have done in Abraham:

Chapter 1: A poem in which all creatures are placed within the natural framework of **a working week**, in order to express the beauty and order of God's handiwork. (More about the Six Days of Creation on page 25.)

Chapters 2-3: A parable in which the basic truths of religion are presented in picture language: that man is the kingpin of creation, that woman is his equal, that marriage is their crowning joy, that God's friendship with human beings was broken and will continue to be broken whenever they assert their independence of God, and that God's reaction to this is to promise that the human race will eventually make good the harm that it has done. (More about Adam and The Garden of Eden on page 25.)

Chapters 4-11: A collection of a number of existing traditions, folklore and legends to illustrate the same basic themes of sin and salvation. Man's original attempt to be his own god leads to greater and greater disaster – from which God rescues him again and again.

The Abraham stories are complemented by traditional stories of Isaac, Jacob and Joseph. They are meant to illustrate how, during the years 1800 to 1500BC God kept the promise he made to Abraham.

Exodus

The book of Exodus continues the story of Abraham's descendants – the Israelites. Some of these had migrated to Egypt during a time of famine. A change in Egypt's political situation threatened to enslave the clan and annihilate it. In fact it was its saving, at a time when its increased numbers already threatened its unity. Under **Moses**, about 1300BC, the disorganised rabble made their escape (that is the meaning of the Greek word *exodos*) in a series of providential happenings that they could never forget. (More about Moses and The Ten Plagues on pages 26-27.)

The Israelite traditions have again been skilfully interwoven to present the marvellous escape in its most dramatic light, as the act in which the God of Abraham intervened in history to keep his promise. This was their **passing-over** from slavery to freedom. The desert journey had welded them together, and at Sinai they came to know the God who had rescued them as '**Yahweh**' – the supreme being who had condescended to enter into a covenant with them, and make them his own people. (More about Passover and Yahweh on pages 27-28.)

It was at Sinai too that the customs which marked them off from other peoples were first organised into a body of religious and civil law. From now on, this would express

God's will for them, the Word of God dwelling with them. To this they dedicated themselves. The ark in which it was placed became the throne of Yahweh, who was on the march with them.

The closing chapters of the book indicate the way in which this basic legislation was afterwards expanded to cover the various details of their later life in Palestine.

Leviticus

Leviticus means 'Priestly'. This book is a collection of the legislation which regulated the priestly worship of Israel after the return from Babylonian exile, about 500BC. This was a time when the community had given up all political ambition, and become again what it had been in the exodus, a Church, cut off from the world, and devoted entirely to the worship of God.

It is this return to the ideals of Moses which makes it fitting that the book should be placed here, under the shadow, as it were, of mount Sinai. Its meticulous concern for cleanness and purity, so disconcerting at first sight, is really a concern that God's people should reflect something of the order which God put into creation, and so make every detail of their lives an act of worship. The book is still used by Jewish children as their first Hebrew reader.

Numbers

The book of Numbers is so called because it begins and ends with the census records traditionally associated with the exodus from Egypt.

Much of the book contains 'priestly' legislation in the spirit of the book of Leviticus. This same spirit has also governed the narrative part of the book (chapters 11 to 24), where the journey through the desert is described as a sort of spiritual retreat. Cut off from the world and alone with God, the Israelites learn, through trial and tension, to know and love the holy God who has come to '**tabernacle**' among them and lead them to the land in which they will find peace. (More about Tabernacle on page 28.)

© UNRWA, M.W. Chaumeny

Deuteronomy

The Greek words *deuteros nomos* mean 'second law'. The legislation it contains is a repetition and expansion of the laws laid down by Moses at mount Sinai, and so is dramatically represented as spoken by him. But Moses's principles have here been warmly re-thought by the prophets who continued his work (especially Hosea, Isaiah and Jeremiah, see below), and adapted to fit the situation of an Israel living in Palestine six hundred years after Moses.

This Israel, often unfaithful to the Sinai covenant, had to be taught to see it as a marriage-contract, binding her to a single-hearted love for the God who had first loved her.

The central code of law in the book (chapters 12 to 26) seems to have been hidden during a time of persecution. Its first publication provided the basis for the important religious reform of king Josiah, about 620BC.

Abraham

The book of Genesis presents Abraham as the father of Isaac and Ishmael. Jews trace their ancestry back to Isaac. Muslims claim Ishmael as their forefather. Both venerate the memory of their common patriarch, Abraham.

The traditions which preserve the memory of some of the important aspects of his life (Genesis 12-23) suggest that he lived in Mesopotamia about 1800BC. His story tells how he was called by God to break all his earthly ties, and set out for the unknown land where he would be alone with God and become the father of a people through whom salvation would come to the whole world.

The Bible praises Abraham's 'faith' in this promise. This refers to his willingness to abandon his own way of thinking and his own human powers, in order to commit himself completely to the word and power of God. This faith is presented as the starting point of mankind's salvation, the beginning of its return journey to God. The disobedience of Adam estranged us from God. Abraham's willing obedience reversed the process. It 'justified' him, says Genesis, that is to say, it put him in the right relationship with God. Faith like Abraham's allows God to do his work in us.

Abraham's faith is tested to the utmost by his willingness to sacrifice his only son (Genesis 22). In response, God makes a covenant with Abraham, and solemnly commits himself to stand by his promise.

The New Testament speaks of the Abraham story as a kind of first draft of the Gospel. It tells us the good news, repeated by Jesus, that anyone showing faith like Abraham's becomes a member of his family, and shares in the promise God made to him.

Scripture foresaw that God would give saving justice to the gentiles through faith. It announced the future gospel to Abraham in the words: 'All nations will be blessed in you.' So it is the people of faith who receive the same blessing as Abraham, the man of faith.
(Galatians 3:8-9)

Six Days of Creation

What a lot of ink has been spilt on this subject! What unnecessary fuss has been caused by people who insist that because it is the Word of God it must be 'true'.

A scientific treatise can be true. A poem can also be true, but in an entirely different way. And this page of Genesis was written by a poet, who sees the world as a vast temple, where the human race can fitly celebrate God's liturgy.

To evoke such a vision, he depends on a primitive science. We call it primitive, but it was everyone's science until comparatively recently. The earth is a flat disc in the centre of the universe. Underneath it is water – you only have to dig to confirm this. Above is more water – as you are reminded every time it rains.

What keeps these two waters separate is the huge vault of the heavens – clearly solid or we'd all be drowned. Across it the heavenly bodies travel – the sun, the moon, and the tiny stars. And the whole complex is covered by a daily alternating veil of darkness and light.

If you wanted to create a world like that, how would you set about it? If you were a poet, you would do it as the author of Genesis 1 has done. The land now separated from the sea must once have been covered by it. The upper and lower waters now separated by the sky must once have enveloped the whole. The recurring darkness of night must have been permanent before light was created.

So the story speaks of the creation of light to separate the spheres of dark and light (day one), the separation of the upper waters from the lower ones (day two), and the separation of the dry land from the sea (day three). The three days that follow are spent furnishing these three compartments – the heavenly bodies (day four), birds and fish (day five), and land animals (day six). Only when this stage is set can the human race appear – the *dramatis personae* for whom the whole was designed.

We need to recognise the artificial nature of this framework, with its contrived harmony and repeated refrain. The existing six-day working week is simply a convenient way of focusing attention on the seventh, the Sabbath.

Nor should we contrast this framework with the one now brought to light by science, either to question scientific discoveries, or to try to reconcile one with the other. Genesis does not concord with science. It deals with entirely different questions. The author is not concerned with *how* the universe came to be, but with *what* the universe is, and *why*. He is concerned to underline its utter dependence on God, its perfection as planned by God, and its subordination to human beings, who have it in their power either to corroborate this designed harmony, or to destroy it.

Adam

Depending on what version of the Old Testament you use, the opening chapters of Genesis may give you the impression that they are speaking of an individual called Adam. But since it is a common literary convention in the Old Testament to collect together the characteristics of a whole race of people under the name of an assumed ancestor, it is more likely that the word *adam* (which is simply the Hebrew for 'man') stands for the whole human race.

In any case, it is clear that the author of these chapters had no access to any information about the individual who may have stood at the beginnings of our history. He was writing about mankind in general. 'The man' in his story plays a representative role. In describing him, the author is describing how every human being stands in relationship to God: utterly dependent on the God who creates him, yet the lord of the rest of creation, a veritable image of God, who calls him into a friendship which will make him a 'son' of God.

Genesis 3 uses the same symbolic language to comment on the fact that human beings reject this call by claiming their own sovereignty in independence of God. They do this not simply as individuals, but as members of a family. Just as there is a community of man, so there is from the very beginnings of our history a community of sin. All those who are born into this community, even before they make their own personal choice, inherit the 'sin of the world' – a complex situation of godlessness and lovelessness from which they need to be saved.

The New Testament will claim that this salvation was accomplished in Jesus. He came as a second Adam, the Son of God and his perfect image, making the invisible God visible to his brothers and sisters. He was born into our sinful situation, and identified himself with our plight, in order to become the representative of a new human race, re-made in that likeness of God which sin destroyed. When God raised him from the dead, a new creation had begun. Believers can share in this by being baptized into the risen Christ, to form the community of those saved from the sin of the world.

The Garden of Eden

The Garden of Eden is a metaphor. This does not mean it can be dismissed. We have to ask what the metaphor stands for.

The author of Genesis 2 is trying to express the happiness of man when there is no sin to place a barrier between himself and God. He has chosen the symbol of a garden. For a nomadic people, depending for its existence upon springs and waterholes, the well-watered soil which produces constant vegetation represents life, security and peace.

This garden he places vaguely 'in the east': he is conscious that his ancestors came into Palestine across the eastern desert from Mesopotamia. *Eden* is actually a Mesopotamian word meaning plain or steppeland. The picture of the Garden of Eden (or better *in* Eden) is therefore of an oasis of fruitfulness and peace in the midst of an unspecified harsh countryside.

The description in Genesis 2:10-14 at first sight seems to give further information on its geographical position. But it is probably a piece of poetic extravagance, suggesting that the garden was so well supplied with water that it could have fed the rivers Euphrates, Tigris, Nile and Indus!

Just as the garden is metaphorical, so also are its trees. The immortality which God intended human beings to enjoy is picturesquely represented as a Tree of Life whose fruit was theirs for the taking. And the forbidden fruit, with its strange title of the Knowledge of Good and Evil, is an obvious symbol of what God must necessarily reserve to himself – the right to determine what is good and what is evil.

For man to seize this right for himself, to determine independently of God what he will call good and what evil, is to set up as a little god of his own. It is this, says our author, that is at the root of all sin. It is this, he says, that inevitably excludes people from the intimacy with God for which they were created. From that moment, the 'cherubim' bar their entrance to the 'garden'.

© John Fisher

The prophets loved to speak of the human longing for the restoration of this friendship with God in terms of re-entering such a garden of fruitfulness and peace (see Isaiah 11:6-9, Ezekiel 34: 25-31). The New Testament claims that this hope of a paradise regained has been answered in the community of Jesus' disciples.

The angel showed me the river of life,
rising from the throne of God and of the Lamb
and flowing crystal-clear.
Down the middle of the city street,
on either bank of the river
were the trees of life,
which bear twelve crops of fruit in a year . . .
and the leaves of which are the cure for the nations.
The curse of destruction will be abolished.
The throne of God and of the Lamb will be in the city;
his servants will worship him,
they will see him face to face . . .
They will not need lamplight or sunlight,
because the Lord their God will be shining on them.
They will reign for ever and ever.
(Revelation 22:1-5)

Moses

There has never been such a prophet in Israel as
Moses, the man whom Yahweh knew face to face.
(Deuteronomy 34:10)

In these words, the Old Testament sums up its admiration for the man upon whom, under God, its faith is founded. If the exodus from Egypt was the most decisive event in Israel's history, then Moses, who was not only responsible for bringing it about, but was also the first to interpret its meaning for his people, cannot but hold a unique position for all time in its annals.

The opening chapters of the book of Exodus try to provide a background. That these pages contain some legendary material is obvious: an attempt is even made to give a Hebrew meaning to his Egyptian name in 2:10. But presumably they also contain some solid historical facts. He was born at a time when the whole of his race had been reduced to slavery. He was providentially given an upbringing which prepared him for his later role as leader of his people. When he had come of age, he retired into the desert from which his forefathers had sprung. There he heard the voice of the 'God of Abraham, Isaac and Jacob', and accepted the call to become the redeemer of Israel (Exodus 3-4).

This redemption consisted not simply in rescuing his people from the clutches of a reluctant Pharaoh (a story dramatically told in Exodus 5-12), nor simply in steering them safely through all the dangers that faced them in the desert (Exodus 13-17). It consisted primarily in bringing the Israelite tribes face to face with God at mount Sinai, so making possible the covenant which transformed them from a motley rabble into the people of God.

Of this covenant between God and Israel, Moses was the mediator. It was his highest achievement. It was through him that Israel saw God, and came to know what he planned for them and demanded of them. Later generations would elaborate the terms of this covenant and adapt them to new circumstances, but always within the framework of the principles Moses had laid down once for all at Sinai. The closing chapters of Exodus, and the rest of the books of the Pentateuch, bear witness to this. Every reform movement that was later to renew Israel had the words 'Back To Moses' as its slogan.

Moses had devoted his life to bringing his people to the promised Land, but he died without setting foot in it. He had so generously identified himself with the desert generation that he suffered their fate. When he was gone, Israel knew that they would need another like him to complete his unfinished work. Deuteronomy 18:18 looks forward to such a one.

The New Testament proclaims that this hope was fully answered in Jesus of Nazareth, the man who had seen God face to face in a way even Moses had not done (John 1:18). Like Moses, he came as a slave among God's people, to redeem them from a servitude of which Egypt was only a symbol (Mark 10:45). Like Moses, he led them through a watery grave (baptism is a share in his death) to a new life beyond (Romans 6:3). Like Moses, he continues to lead them through a lifetime of hardship, where the Word of God is their guide, and the Bread from heaven their food (John 6). Like Moses, he grants them a vision of God, but they must be content to see God through his eyes until they reach the promised Kingdom (John 14:9).

The Gospels of Matthew and John lay strong emphasis on this role of Jesus as a new Moses. The Easter liturgy develops the theme with enthusiasm.

The Ten Plagues

For the Israelites, the exodus from Egypt was the supreme example of God's faithfulness to his promise to save his people. No one should be surprised, therefore, that the traditions which told and retold the story of this event should have taken on the air of an epic.

All the emphasis has been placed on the miraculous and the extraordinary. The ordinary secondary causes have been by-passed, in order to allow the essence of the matter to stand out more clearly. Why did all these things happen? 'So that you will know that there is no one like Yahweh our God' (Exodus 8:10).

The plague of Egypt formed part of this epic. Anyone who compares Psalm 78, Psalm 105, Wisdom 11 and Wisdom 16, will discover that there was much freedom and variation in the telling of the stories. The editor of Exodus 7-12 has dramatised the story even more by combining all the traditional stories into a round ten:

1. Water turned into blood.
2. Swarm of frogs.
3. Swarm of mosquitoes.
4. Swarm of horseflies.
5. Cattle pest.
6. Sores and boils.
7. Hail.
8. Swarm of locusts.
9. Darkness.
10. Death of the first-born.

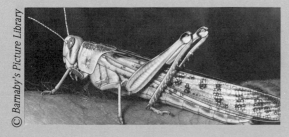

© Barnaby's Picture Library

This series the Egyptian magicians find it increasingly difficult to imitate. Each prodigy is the direct reply to the Pharaoh's repeated failure to honour his promise to release the enslaved Israelites. By this means, the author has dramatically raised the tension. When the tenth plague is reached, there should be no doubt left in the reader's mind that nothing will stop God from bringing about his declared plan.

It is this theological lesson alone which should claim our attention when we read these chapters, since this alone was the intention of the author. Not much purpose is served by pointing out that most of these plagues occur 'naturally'

every year, during Egypt's spring floods and summer heat. They do indeed, and one can safely assume that a television camera would not have recorded the events in the same way that the book of Exodus has done.

But the author of Exodus is not concerned with producing a mere video of the events. His purpose is to reveal to men and women of faith the hand of God shaping all events, whether they are supernatural or 'only natural'.

The author of the book of Revelation has the same purpose when he describes the 'natural' calamities of his own time in terms of the Egyptian plagues. His readers too must see them as signs that God is here and now present in our history, to save those he has promised to save (Revelation 15-16).

Passover

Nobody knows the origins of the Passover festival. It is a reasonable guess that it began as a springtime ritual in Israel's shepherd days. To acknowledge the supreme rights of God over the first-born of man and beast, a lamb was offered in sacrifice and eaten, and its blood smeared on the doorway of the tent (or later of the house) to indicate that the ceremony had been duly performed. The Hebrew name *pesach* means 'jump' and perhaps referred to the ritual dance that accompanied this sacrifice.

Later, when the Israelites became an agricultural people, an offering of the first-fruits of the harvest was added to this animal sacrifice. So unleavened bread would be eaten with the paschal lamb, to express utter dependence on God for both the fruit of the land and the fruit of the womb. No sanctuary, altar or priest was required for this religious ceremony.

This ritual acquired an entirely new significance during the exodus from Egypt, which took place while the Israelites were celebrating it. An epidemic had struck their Egyptian slavemasters, and created the confusion which finally allowed them to make their escape to freedom. The epidemic was interpreted as God's punishment on the pagan people whose unbloody doors showed that they did not acknowledge his supremacy over their first-born.

Yet the destruction had 'jumped' or 'passed over' the name of Israel in the list of those who were doomed. This was seen as a sign that in these events Israel had become God's own first-born. Ever after, the feast would mark the birthday of Israel as God's own people. The word Passover would remind them of the night in which they had passed over from slavery into freedom. This is still the meaning it has for all Jews.

It had that meaning for Jesus too. He died at the time of the Passover feast, and he celebrated it in a home-setting with his friends the night before he died. His words at that last supper state that people need to be freed from a slavery worse than Egypt's before they can fully pass into the presence of God.

The New Testament claims that Jesus was the true paschal Lamb (John 1:29, Revelation 5:6), in whose night of death and resurrection the new Israel was born (1 Corinthians 5:7). The Christian paschal feast of Easter celebrates and renews this faith.

Yahweh

The name Yahweh does not appear in most translations of the Bible. Since it was regarded as the proper name of God, the Jews had already, out of reverence, substituted for it the title *Adonai*, which means 'The Lord'. Most translations have followed this custom.

To remind the Jewish reader to say 'Adonai' where the word 'Yahweh' was written, the vowels of the first (a, o, a) were placed into the written consonants of the second. This gave rise to the hybrid word 'Yahowah' or 'Jehovah' when the purpose of the vowel-change was no longer understood.

Nonetheless the consonants of the name Yahweh appears in the Hebrew text of the Old Testament about six thousand times. The traditions it contains do not agree about when and how it was first made known to Israel. One tradition (Genesis 4:26) puts the event as far back as the antediluvian patriarchs.

But it seems most probable that the name was not in use before the time of Moses. According to Exodus 3:13-14, he asked for the name of the God who was sending him to rescue his enslaved brothers in Egypt. The name would give him some information about such a God. The name, he is told, is 'Yahweh'. The text goes on to explain that this is an abbreviation for *yahweh asher yahweh*, 'he is who he is'.

These words have sometimes been interpreted as a revelation of God's infinite being – 'He is a being whose essence is to be'. But it is quite improbable that the Hebrew mind could have intended or understood anything so metaphysical. The sentence reads far more naturally as a straight refusal on the part of God to reveal his name or give himself away.

Yet this refusal is not merely negative. God declines to define himself, not because he does not want to, but because he cannot. He is above definition. He cannot – as other gods might – be tied down to a description.

The name Yahweh is meant to remind God's people for all time of their powerlessness to penetrate the transcendence of God. People who talk or act as if they knew exactly what God is or what his plans are, have got it wrong. 'He is' what he is. He cannot be expressed. He is the unspeakable mystery.

Tabernacle

The word tabernacle is Latin for 'tent'. It is the name given in our English Bibles to the portable temple used by the Israelites in their nomadic exodus from Egypt. Like their own tents, it could be dismantled and transported, to be set up in any new encampment that they chose.

The Old Testament speaks of it variably as the Tent of the Dwelling (of God), or the Tent of Meeting (with God). It was designed to house the ark of the covenant, the symbol of God's presence among his people, a pilgrim among fellow pilgrims, leading them in their march to the land he had promised them.

John's Gospel will later state that this religious theme finds its fullest meaning in Jesus, whose life was a living expression of the fact that God had 'pitched his tent among us' (John 1:14). The receptacle in which the Eucharist is reserved in many churches has often been made in the shape of a tent, and is still called the tabernacle.

We have no accurate information on the structure and furnishing of the desert tabernacle. The detailed description given in Exodus 26 and 36 is an idealised one, influenced (understandably enough) by the later Jerusalem temple which eventually fulfilled the same function for an Israel that was no longer nomadic.

2. The Writing of the Law

We have now seen something of what the 'Law of Moses' contains. But we also need to know how it came to be written, since this will influence the way we understand it.

It has already been suggested, several times, that however much Moses may have had to do with these five books, he couldn't have written them in the form we now have them. Indeed, a child could point out that a book which contains an account of Moses' death (Deuteronomy 34) was presumably not written by him. Or that books which regularly use the phrase 'before there were kings in Israel' could not have been written before the monarchy was instituted three hundred years after Moses. Or that passages which keep referring to the south as 'towards the desert', and the west as 'towards the sea', could not have been written in Egypt, but only in Palestine, which Moses never reached.

But it is not only these minor details that have made scholars question the tradition which has fathered these five books on to Moses. It is above all the duplication and repetition of material, referred to above, which would be very strange indeed coming from the hand of a single author. Right from the opening pages, it is odd to read in Genesis 2 that Yahweh (the Lord) shaped a man out of the clay soil and breathed life into him, when we have already read in chapter 1 the story of man's creation by Elohim (God). A few chapters further on, when the Flood is being described, for some strange reason, Yahweh notices the wickedness of the human race, and then Elohim notices the wickedness of the human race. Noah enters the Ark with the animals two by two, and then he enters with the animals seven by seven. The Flood comes twice, and it stops twice, once after forty days, and the second time after hundred and fifty days. In Genesis 27, Jacob unwillingly leaves Palestine to stay with his uncle in Syria, scared by the anger of his brother Esau. In the following chapter, the same uncle lives in Mesopotamia, and Jacob goes there with the best will in the world: he's looking for a wife.

The examples could be multiplied. When closer examination reveals that these duplicated stories are regularly distinct from each other in vocabulary and style, and regularly use different names for God, then the text almost invites us to recognise that it cannot be the work of one hand. It seems to be a complex sewing together of several different sources and traditions. The Law turns out to be not Mosaic, but a mosaic.

Most scholars now agree that the 'five books of Moses' are in fact the bringing together of four distinct sources, all of them rooted in the exodus event of which they speak, but not written down until centuries after Moses, and not edited into their present form until 350 years before Christ. They have been given the titles J, E, D and P.

The Yahwist

J stands for the **Yahwistic** tradition, so called because it gives God the name Yahweh (Jahveh) throughout. All the most colourful and memorable stories in these books are from the Yahwist. Read his account of Abraham bargaining with God in Genesis 18, or of Isaac's meeting with Rebekah in Genesis 24, or of Jacob seeking his father's blessing in Genesis 27.

The Yahwist is not much interested in legislation: he records only the commandments of Exodus 34. But neither is he simply an entertaining storyteller. His stories are deeply theological. Yahweh is a God with whom people can feel at ease: in Genesis 2-3 he is not only a potter, but also a gardener, and a householder, and a surgeon, and a judge, and a tailor. Yet beware anyone who tries to be his equal – that was precisely Adam's sin! And yet again, Yahweh knows how weak we humans are, and human failings quickly evoke his pity – for Adam in Genesis 3, for Cain in Genesis 4, and even in the disaster of the Flood 'Noah won Yahweh's favour' (Genesis 6).

The Yahwist's story, as far as we can reconstruct it, is generally optimistic in tone. It seems to reflect the enthusiasm of Israel's youth in the early days of the monarchy, and was perhaps first put into writing about 950BC.

The Elohist

E stands for the **Elohistic** tradition, which prefers to call God Elohim, a plural of majesty and transcendence. Such a God does not sit under a tree to chat with his friends. He speaks to people in theophanies so mind-blowing that the very ground he walks on becomes sacred (Exodus 3), or even more remotely, in dreams (see the Joseph story in Genesis 37-50). Such a God cannot be represented. Indeed the name Yahweh, first revealed to Moses, is explained as 'The Inexpressible Mystery'.

This more sophisticated theology is echoed by a more refined morality. Abraham no longer tells Sarah to pretend she is his sister as in Genesis 12 (J), but actually *is* his half-sister (Genesis 20). Jacob no longer cheats to rob his uncle Laban as in Genesis 30 (J), but is simply assisted by God (Genesis 31). And so on. The legislation contained in this tradition (Exodus 21-23) is remarkable in its concern for justice and moderation. Retaliation of only 'an eye for an eye' (Exodus 21:24) is a considerable improvement upon Lamech's demand of a 77-fold vengeance in Genesis 4:24 (J).

The generally pessimistic tone of E reflects the preaching of the early prophets and their fight against an encroaching paganism in order to recall Israel back to its desert purity. It was probably put into writing in the more austere and Moses-conscious northern kingdom, about 800BC.

The Deuteronomist

D stands for the **Deuteronomic** tradition, and it is given this name because it is to be found almost exclusively in the book of Deuteronomy. It contains no stories, only legislation. Yet far from this making the book a cold one, it is the warmest of the five.

The book is a meditation on Israel's history. Why did God chose the Israelites? Because they deserved it? Not at all. It was out of sheer love. Why had God protected them throughout their story? Out of sheer love. Why had God continued to heap on them so many blessings? Out of sheer love. Read chapter 7.

© Barnaby's Picture Library

This love of God calls for a response. Israel's obedience to God's laws can no longer be seen as a burdensome duty, only as a return of love for love – love for God, and love for neighbour, even for the stranger in the midst. Some of the book's most moving pages are concerned with the protection of the weak (see chapter 24).

This passionate tone echoes the preaching of the later prophets, with all their experience of Israel's infidelity under its successive kings. The emphasis is again on a return to the principles of Moses, though this is expressed in legislation adapted to much later times. The most distinctive piece of legislation is the restriction of worship to a single sanctuary (chapter 12), where J and E had allowed for several. Such legislation was not in force until the year 620BC. The book itself can be dated about 700BC. It had a profound effect on the books of Joshua-Judges-Samuel-Kings, which were written by the same editors.

The Priests

P stands for the **Priestly** tradition. It is so called because it concentrates almost entirely on matters of liturgy, priesthood and worship. Its tone is inevitably dry, technical and cold. Test this by reading Genesis 5 or Exodus 25-31.

Here the history of Israel is told again, from Adam down to the present, but this time as the story of a holy community bound to God by successive covenants – with Adam, with Noah, and with Abraham. These covenants are linked to each other in an orderly manner, and everything that can be listed and counted is listed and counted.

The story comes to a climax in the great law-giver Moses, and the covenant God established through him at Sinai. Moses's legislation for the simple worship conducted in the desert is made the basis for the more complex legislation which later regulated the Jerusalem priesthood and temple. This fills the closing chapters of Exodus, the whole of Leviticus, and the opening chapters of Numbers.

The tradition contains plenty of stories, but only to draw attention to pieces of legislation. The story of the six-day creation is told only to throw the seventh day Sabbath into relief (Genesis 1). The story of Abraham is told only to emphasise the law of circumcision (Genesis 17), on which J and E say nothing. The story of the plagues of Egypt is told only to stress the rubrics to be followed at Passover (Exodus 12).

This meticulous emphasis on legislation makes the Priestly tradition far colder than J, E or D. Yet it has a power of its own, with its overwhelming emphasis on a God who is transcendent, unapproachable, holy, 'different'. That such a God has pitched his tent among the Israelites demands that they too be holy and 'different'. 'Be holy, for I, Yahweh your God, am holy' is its repeated watchword.

Such a deeply spiritual concept was not evolved in Israel until the time of its exile in Babylonia, under the influence of the priest-prophet Ezekiel, about 540BC. It had a profound effect on the books of Chronicles-Ezra-Nehemiah, which were written by the same editors.

The four traditions that we have analysed above, J, E, D and P, are entirely parallel to one another. They deal with the same basic events, but each from a distinct viewpoint. To distinguish them as we have done would seem at first to diminish the stature of Moses. In fact it does the opposite. It has emphasised the importance of Moses as the supreme legislator, to whom all future ages would look back.

The stature of the Law is increased even more. It is no longer merely a record of the past, a sort of porridge in which everything is of the same grey consistency. It is a collection of all that is finest in Israel's tradition, from one end of its history to the other. This will be for ever afterwards the Jewish Torah or guide for living, the yardstick by which every Jew measures his life. Even Jesus did so, for his mission was not to supersede the Law, but to bring it to perfection (Matthew 5:17-19).

The book of Nehemiah describes the impact made on the people when one of the first editions of the four traditions was read out to them:

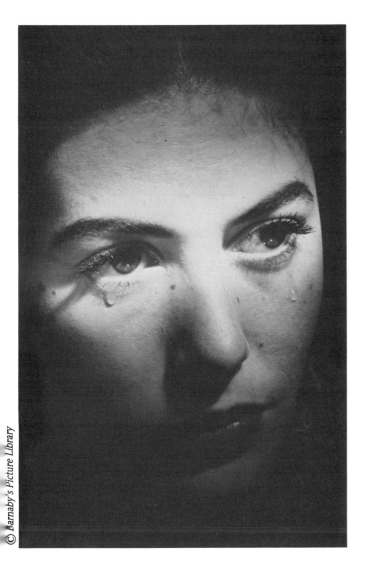

© Barnaby's Picture Library

B. The Prophets

The second section of the Old Testament is called The Prophets. It begins not with Isaiah and Jeremiah, but with Joshua, Judges, Samuel and Kings. This in itself is significant. It is we who called these books 'historical', and took them as a straightforward account of events. The Jews (and they after all wrote them) call them 'The Prophets', that is, the work of the prophetical movement, a prophetical meditation on past events in order to draw a religious meaning out of them. The right approach to these books demands that we treat them as such.

> Give heed, my people, to my teaching;
> turn your ear to the words of my mouth.
> I will open my mouth in a parable
> and reveal hidden lessons of the past.
> (Psalm 78:1-2, GV)

What is the 'parable' which the psalmist then goes on to tell? Simply the story of Israel from the exodus down to the time of king David. For the Old Testament, that story is not told in order to keep a record of the past. It is a parable which contains a profound lesson. To seize on the historical aspect of this story and to tie oneself into knots in an attempt to reconcile its inconsistencies, out of a sense of reverence for the authors, is sheer stupidity if the authors never intended it to be taken as straight history. They wrote not to inform their readers, but to move them, to console them, and to convert them.

The authors of Joshua-Judges-Samuel-Kings, then, look back on the story of Israel, from the end of the exodus down to the eve of the Babylonian exile, and offer their interpretation of the sequence of events. They write in the spirit of Deuteronomy, and are best understood if read alongside the books of Hosea, Isaiah and Jeremiah, whose preaching they echo.

Their theme throughout is that Israel's past is the love story of a God who cannot abide his 'bride' to have any other lovers but himself. Failure to realise this inevitably brings God's plans for Israel to ruin.

The people were all in tears as they listened to the words of the Law ... Ezra said to them, 'Today is sacred to our Lord. Do not be sad: the joy of Yahweh is your stronghold.' ... Then all the people went off to eat and drink and give helpings away and enjoy themselves to the full, since they had understood the meaning of what had been proclaimed to them.
(Nehemiah 8:9-12)

Things to do . . .

Take a story told by all four evangelists (Matthew, Mark, Luke and John), and edit them into a single account which incorporates all the details. What have you gained? What have you lost?

Divide your discussion group into four sub-groups called J, E, D and P. Each sub-group has to find material in the Pentateuch expressing its own distinctive style and interest (D will be the easiest!) Report back to the large group and discuss.

Joshua

The book is named after its hero, Moses's lieutenant, whose blitzkrieg brought the exodus to a successful conclusion and led the Israelite tribes into Palestine about 1250BC. Around his name have been gathered a vast assortment of ancient traditions which, although not always agreeing with each other in detail, nevertheless enthusiastically convey the conviction that the God of the covenant keeps his word, and overcomes all obstacles to give his people the Kingdom he promises them. Through Joshua, the God of mount Sinai was successfully enthroned in the land of Palestine.

The Greek form of Joshua's name, which means saviour, is Jesus. The early Christian writers were delighted with this coincidence. They saw Jesus as completing what his namesake had only begun, and leading God's people into that promised Land of which Palestine was only a pale figure.

Judges

The Hebrew word 'to judge' implies more than the legalistic passing of a judgement between truth and error, or right and wrong. It means to condemn evil in a practical way by rescuing the innocent from the clutches of villains. The title

© Barnaby's Picture Library

of Judge was therefore given to those leaders of the Israelite people who defended them against oppression in the critical years after they had entered Palestine, from 1200 to 1050BC.

The book of Judges, though it deals with the same conquest of Palestine, is less enthusiastic than Joshua. But it may be more realistic in its description of the long struggle of the Israelite tribes to maintain their independence. Nor is there much connection between the popular traditions that grew up around the leaders of the scattered tribes – Othniel, Ehud, Deborah, Gideon, Jephthah and **Samson**. (More about Samson on page 38.) But all of them are meant to illustrate the faith that God's people prosper only as long as they remain faithful to him. The Kingdom is always eluding their grasp because they are weak. But their cry for help is to a God who is willing to forgive 'seventy times seven'.

Samuel and Kings

The four books of Samuel and Kings deal with five hundred years of Israel's history, from about 1050 to 550BC. It was a time when the temporary weakness of neighbouring nations allowed the founding of a strong and independent kingdom in Palestine. But a schism rendered Israel itself weaker, and when the world powers of Egypt, Assyria and Babylonia eventually began their struggle for domination, the Israelites could not avoid being embroiled, and finally almost eliminated.

To cover this period, the authors of these books have made use of the historical materials available to them. Through them, they try to present a picture of the conditions and difficulties of establishing a Kingdom of God on earth.

The two books of Samuel are based on some of the Old Testament's most vivid records. They tell of the crisis about 1050BC which accentuated Israel's need for a hereditary king, of Samuel the last of the Judges and his hesitations, of Saul the first king and his failure to live up to the ideals Samuel had proposed, and of the gradual establishment of **David** as ruler over a united kingdom. (More about David on page 38.)

The records on which the authors have relied focus considerable attention on David's capture of Jerusalem, and of his success in installing the Ark of the Covenant there. Enthroned at the right hand of this symbol of God's presence, and thus making visible God's invisible kingship over his people, David is seen as the fulfilment of God's plan for Israel.

The two books of Kings have used less interesting material, largely the state annals of the two kingdoms into which Israel eventually schismatically divided. Yet through this unpromising material, the authors have made their lesson clearest of all. **Solomon's** story focuses on the building of the **Temple** (more about Solomon and the Temple on page 39) which is to house the Ark, the one source of Israel's well-being. But his unfaithfulness to this ideal leads to the gradual decline of the kingdom, and each of his successors, whatever his good faith, is condemned for his failure to return to the ideal. Two only are praised – Hezekiah and Josiah – for their efforts at religious reform.

It was a time for prophets to arise to recall Israel to its first principles, and the sagas of **Elijah and Elisha** are lovingly told. (More about Elijah and Elisha on page 40.) But even the prophetical movement failed to avert the impending disaster. The fall of Samaria in the eighth century BC, and of Jerusalem in the sixth, was a judgement of God. Sin destroys the Kingdom, and God's people must go into exile.

And yet, typically, this Deuteronomic history does not end on a merely negative note. Read 2 Kings 25:27-30. Does it leave you hopeful?

The Prophets Proper

In ordinary usage, the word 'prophecy' means the prediction of something that has not yet taken place. In this sense there are remarkably few 'prophecies' of the New Testament in the Old. Almost all of the texts, even those which do have some reference to the future, prove on closer examination to refer more immediately to contemporary events. For the prophets were not simply *foretellers* of the future, in such a way as would make the Old and New Testaments simply two halves of an equation. They are rather to be thought of as *forthtellers*, proclaiming God's will and purpose to the people of their own generation, and appealing for their faith and commitment. Certainly they express hopes for the *future* fulfilment of God's plans. But this is for the same purpose as their meditation on God's self-revelation in the *past*, to focus both on the needs of the *present*.

© Associated Press

The first and greatest of these men was Moses, who interpreted to the Israelites the meaning of their exodus from Egypt as the moment in which they became the people of God, bound to him by solemn covenant. The books of Samuel and Kings tell how a group of prophets tried to keep this vision before Israel's eyes during the critical years after the conquest of Palestine. The movement, at first rather primitive, professional and frankly political, was gradually purified by figures like Elijah and Elisha, to produce from about 750BC onward the series of great men whose preaching has been preserved in writing.

All of these saw themselves as champions of the religion of Sinai. Their mission was to drive home its deepest implications to a people prone to be content with externals and to reduce God to the level of the Canaanite idols. When their preaching is read out, it is not to inform people about past history and theology, but to allow them, if they are prone to the same idolatry, to share these ever relevant insights into the reality of God.

The prophetical books were not generally written by the named prophets themselves. More usually they consist of excerpts from their preaching, collected, edited, and sometimes added to after their death by their disciples. The sequence of thought does not therefore run from one chapter into the next; sometimes it is restricted to a few verses only. An edition of the Bible with subheadings is an enormous help in this respect.

The order in which the books have been printed in our Bible is based simply on their length and importance. Here they have been rearranged, for convenience, into chronological order.

Amos

The first prophet whose preaching has come down to us in writing is Amos. He lived about 750BC (see 2 Kings 14), at a time when the northern kingdom of Israel was enjoying a final period of prosperity, and complacently congratulating itself on having a God who was so patently pleased with the nation. Amos's vocation was to prick this bubble.

Such a nationalist and private God, served by a self-satisfied Israel, was not the God who had revealed himself to Moses. The God of Sinai was the one and only God, the God of justice who ruled over all people, and demanded their whole-hearted service. His covenant with the Israelites, far from demanding less from them, demanded more. Their failure to meet these demands would be punished by the Assyrian invasion. The book finishes with the hope of the emergence of a truer Israel.

You alone have I intimately known of all the families of oarth, that is why I shall punish you for all your wrong-doings.

(Amos 3:1)

Hosea

A contemporary of Amos, Hosea provides the necessary balance to his fierce message by showing that God is a God of love. This he preaches not only in word but in action, through his own heartbroken love for his wayward wife Gomer. The Sinai covenant was a marriage bond. Unfaithfulness to it is a sort of adultery, wounding the heart of a loving God.

This does not mean that God will just forgive and forget: Hosea can never forget Gomer, even when he sends her into purdah. But the apparent punishment is only a ruse to re-awaken love. In the same way, Hosea hopes, the imminent deportation to Assyria will be a sort of return to the Sinai desert, where God can re-create the lovableness of his bride. He was too optimistic. The deportees never came back.

The New Testament will use the same bold metaphor of marriage and the desert to illustrate the relationship of God with his people, consummated in Christ.

*I am going to seduce her
and lead her into the desert
and speak to her heart.*

(Hosea 2:16)

Isaiah 1-39

Isaiah, the most outstanding of the prophets, exercised his ministry in Jerusalem from 740 to 690BC (see 2 Kings 15-20). These were years during which Assyria began its expansion south towards Egypt, and (as Amos and Hosea had warned) eliminated the northern kingdom of Israel that stood in the way. In these circumstances, the southern kingdom of Judah was itself tempted to rely on political and military means to protect itself. It was against this background that Isaiah preached the God of holiness and transcendence, the master of history. Any attempt to control one's own destiny was sheer blasphemy, a rejection of the God revealed at Sinai, who demanded blind and absolute faith in himself alone. Isaiah's very name spelt this out. It means 'Salvation comes from Yahweh.'

The obedience of king Hezekiah to these ideals made Isaiah hail him, in the famous chapters 7-12, as an **immanu-El** (more about Immanuel on page 40) an illustration of the truth that God is on our side, and so a first sketch of the kind of leader through whom God saves his people. The miraculous preservation of Jerusalem in the Assyrian advance of the year 701 confirmed these hopes of Isaiah.

> *If you will not take your stand on me*
> *you will not stand firm.*
>
> (literally) *If you do not say Amen to me*
> *you can say Amen.*
>
> *(Isaiah 7:9)*

Only the first 39 chapters of this book (with some exceptions) represent the preaching of Isaiah of Jerusalem. On the rest of the book, see page 36 and 37 below.

Micah

Micah was a contemporary of Isaiah. Against the same background of political intrigue, he preached the same need for the sort of faith which commits itself entirely into God's hands. Disobedience will bring on Judah the divine judgement recently passed on Israel. Only blind obedience, like that of Hezekiah, can bring the ideal descendant of David who will deliver his people from their enemies, and give them a lasting peace.

> *In the days to come . . .*
> *nation will not lift sword against nation*
> *or ever again be trained to make war.*
>
> *(Micah 4:3)*

Zephaniah

This prophet witnessed one of the blackest periods in Judah's history (see 2 Kings 21), when the Assyrian Empire which had engulfed it demanded tribute not only in money but also in religious practice, and all the paganism fought by the prophets had returned.

Zephaniah could see only doom for his people on the coming Day of the Lord, except for the humble and the poor who, accepting their impoverishment by the invaders, turned to God with nothing in their hands. Luke's Gospel

© UNRWA

will describe Mary, and indeed all candidates for God's Kingdom, in the same terms.

> *Zion, have no fear . . .*
> *Yahweh your God is in your midst (*literally, *in your*
> *womb),*
> *the warrior-Saviour.*
>
> *(Zephaniah 3:16-17)*

Nahum

Nahum sounds the same note of doom as his predecessor Zephaniah, but the doom is for the Assyrian Empire, which at the height of its glory began to show signs of crumbling. With passionate and ironic joy, he looks forward to the impending ruin of its capital Nineveh (612BC), the cruel persecutor of God's people which must be regarded as the arch-enemy of God. The book of Jonah will disagree (see below page 37).

> *Disaster to the city of blood . . .*
> *the graceful beauty, the cunning witch,*
> *who enslaved nations by her harlotries.*
>
> *(Nahum 3:1-4)*

Jeremiah

2 Kings 22-25 tells of the years 640 to 590BC. It was a time of political and religious chaos for the kingdom of Judah, as the Assyrian Empire gave way to the Babylonian, and the continued intrigue of Judah's kings finally brought about the destruction of Jerusalem and the deportation of the nation into exile. Jeremiah's vocation was to foretell this ruin of his country.

The book which contains his preaching is strewn with pieces of biography written in the third person, and with fragments of a personal diary written in the first person. These reveal him to us as a man of a deeply sensitive nature, torn constantly between his love for his people and his loyalty to the God who gave him only a message of doom to preach to them – a message which is still known today as a 'jeremiad'. Such a commission brought him misunderstanding, loneliness, and eventually rejection as a traitor. Yet he was recognised in later years as a truer patriot than his short-sighted contemporaries, and honoured as one of Israel's greatest saints (see 2 Maccabees 15:10-16).

His immense suffering had forced Jeremiah to turn to God as his only consolation. And in this process of being stripped of all other support, he understood more deeply than any of his predecessors the true nature of God. In giving this deeper understanding to a nation that was shortly to be stripped in the same way, Jeremiah was later seen as a foreshadowing of Jesus, the man of sorrows who saves his people by his passion and death. Indeed, even Jesus' contemporaries seem to have seen in him another Jeremiah (see Matthew 16:14).

In the important chapters 29-33, Jeremiah looks forward to the joy of the new covenant which God will make with those who have learnt this lesson of spiritual poverty.

> A voice is heard in Ramah, lamenting and weeping
> bitterly:
> it is Rachel weeping for her children . . .
> because they are no more.
> Yahweh says this:
> Stop your lamenting, dry your eyes . . .
> they will return from the enemy's country.
> *(Jeremiah 31:15-16)*

Habakkuk

About the beginning of the Babylonian exile which brought such anguish to our Old Testament ancestors, the prophet Habakkuk makes an attempt to solve the problem of evil. He sees that the invasion of Judah by the Babylonians, dramatically represented as still in the future, was a fitting punishment for centuries of disobedience. But he asks why God should have used for this purpose a nation even more culpable than Judah.

The only answer he can find is that God's ways are a mystery to the human mind, which must continue by faith to crucify its self-sufficiency if it is to find life. The short book finishes with a canticle of certainty that God will vindicate such faith.

> Anyone whose heart is not upright will succumb,
> but the upright will live through faithfulness.
> *(Habakkuk 3:4)*

Ezekiel

Ezekiel ministered to his people at a critical juncture in their history. Deported to Babylon at the beginning of the exile about 600BC, it fell to him to maintain the faith of the Jews when the disaster which his predecessors had only threatened was actually taking place. For this task he admitted that he was entirely inadequate: he continually calls himself a mere 'son of man', and can only appeal to the meaning of his own name *yehezek-El*, 'It is God who gives strength'. In this strength he preached to his fellow exiles that the deportation was no mere temporary setback, but a lifetime in which Judaism must change its ideas. This message occupies the first half of the book, told for the large part in brilliant mime.

In the second half, when the eventual fall of Jerusalem had frozen the exiles into apathy, he rallies them with his brilliant parable of a dead Judaism rising again from its graveyard, and his fantastic plans for rebuilding the Jerusalem temple, a vision which was to influence deeply the description of the New Jerusalem in the closing pages of the New Testament (Revelation 21-22).

Ezekiel's priestly ideal of a people transformed by the exile, and henceforward finding in the service of God the only reason for their existence, made him the father of late Judaism, and had a profound influence on the authors of Leviticus (see page 24 above) and Chronicles-Ezra-Nehemiah (see page 45 below).

> 'Son of man, can these bones lives?'
> I said, 'You know, Lord Yahweh.'
> He said, 'Prophesy over these bones,
> say, "Dry bones, hear the word of Yahweh".'
> *(Ezekiel 37:3-4)*

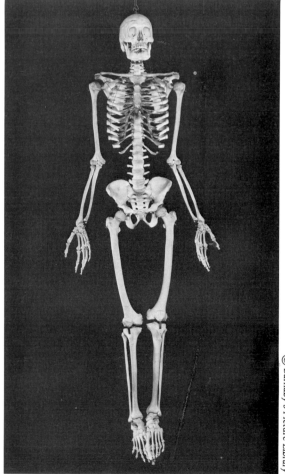

© Barnaby's Picture Library

Isaiah 40-55

These chapters of the book of Isaiah are perhaps the best known in the whole Old Testament. Anyone who has ever heard Handel's *Messiah* will know the opening paragraphs by heart, through the arias 'Comfort ye', 'Every valley', 'O thou that tellest' and 'He will feed his flock'. The chapters contain the preaching of a school of Isaiah's disciples who, 150 years after their master was dead, continued to apply his principles to new circumstances, and to offer their consolation to the exiles of Babylon. The background presumes that the Babylonian rule is over, and that the Persian Cyrus (he is actually named twice) is here and now inviting the exiles to embark on an exodus even more marvellous than the first, to a renewed Jerusalem.

This book of Consolation, as it is known, is punctuated by four remarkable poems which speak of a **Suffering Servant**. (More about the Suffering Servant on page 41.) They present dramatically Isaiah's ideal of an Israel placing itself completely in God's hands, willing even to undergo death in order to bring the knowledge of God to a pagan world. Only such an Israel will be worthy to enter the new Jerusalem. The New Testament will make much of these poems. So will Handel.

> *He was despised, the lowest of men,*
> *a man of sorrows, familiar with suffering.*
>
> *(Isaiah 53:3)*

© UNRWA, M. Nasr

Haggai

Haggai ministered to the Jews during the years immediately following their return from exile about 540BC. In spite of their disappointment over the difficulties of post-war reconstruction, he felt it essential that they should set about the rebuilding of the temple on which the exile prophets had placed such emphasis (see Ezra 1-6).

The four addresses of Haggai that have been preserved are all concerned with this project, and his promise that this second temple would surpass even Solomon's when it was graced with the presence of God.

> *The glory of this new temple*
> *will surpass that of the old,*
> *says Yahweh Sabaoth.*
>
> *(Haggai 2:9)*

Zechariah 1-8

A contemporary of Haggai, Zechariah also worked for the rebuilding of the temple. He insisted that the holiness it represented must be echoed in the people, if the salvation they longed for was not to be held up any longer. In eight visions, he shows how constantly God has proved his readiness to save: the coming of the Kingdom depends upon ourselves.

> *Sing, rejoice, daughter of Zion,*
> *for now I am coming*
> *to live among you.*
>
> *(Zechariah 2:14)*

Only the first eight chapters of this book represent the preaching of Zechariah himself. On the concluding six chapters, see page 37 below.

Malachi

Malachi lived about 450BC, at the time of the great reformers Ezra and Nehemiah. The enthusiasm aroused in 515BC by the rebuilding of the temple had now petered out. In its place there was deadness and apathy, reflected in the careless formalism of religious practice, and in the lax acceptance of divorce and mixed marriage (see the books of Ezra and Nehemiah, page 45 below).

Malachi places the main blame for this laxity on the priesthood. He hopes for a time when a reformed priesthood will offer worthy sacrifice to a God who has finally returned to his temple.

> *Why does one of you not close the doors*
> *and so stop the pointless lighting of fires on my altar?*
> *I am not pleased with you, says Yahweh Sabaoth.*
>
> *(Malachi 1:10)*

Joel

Like his contemporary Malachi, Joel sees the careless performance of the liturgy as the greatest obstacle to the coming of God's Kingdom. For him, the devastation caused by a plague of locusts is a judgement of God, calling on his people to acknowledge their need for repentance. It is only such 'lenten' repentance that will ultimately lead to the defeat of God's enemies, and to the 'pentecostal' outpouring of the Spirit, in which God comes to dwell with his people (see Acts 2:17-21).

> *Come back to me with all your heart,*
> *fasting, weeping, mourning.*
> *Tear your hearts and not your clothes,*
> *and come back to Yahweh your God.*
>
> *(Joel 2:12)*

Obadiah

The single chapter of this book deals with a single theme, the punishment of the treacherous Edomites who, far from coming to the aid of their Israelite kinsmen in their hour of need, had contributed to the destruction of Jerusalem in 586BC.

The theme is based on the justice of a God who will not allow the enemies of his people to go unpunished. Other contemporary prophets will draw attention to God's mercy.

> *Though you soar like an eagle,*
> *though you set your nest among the stars,*
> *I shall bring you down from there!*
> *declares Yahweh.*
>
> *(Obadiah 4)*

Isaiah 56-66

These chapters contain a variety of material connected with the name of Isaiah of Jerusalem. Some pieces may go back to the period before exile, perhaps to the prophet Isaiah himself. Others are reminiscent of the hopes expressed during exile in Isaiah 40-55 (see above page 36). But the bulk of these chapters come from a school of Isaiah's disciples belonging to the fifth century post-exile reform movement.

Like Malachi and Joel, they underline the nation's need for self-criticism. But they also censure the narrow and exclusive outlook of the reformers, and urge a return to the more universal views of the master Isaiah, of an Israel no longer at daggers drawn with the gentiles, but leading them to God.

> *No foreigner adhering to Yahweh should say,*
> *'Yahweh will utterly exclude me from his people.'*
>
> *(Isaiah 56:3)*

Jonah

The little book of Jonah illustrates the same universal outlook. This is in danger of being missed by those only concerned with defending the story's historicity, for whom the whale has swallowed not only Jonah but the whole book.

The story is not a piece of history at all but, in the nature of *Gulliver's Travels* a bitter political satire on the nationalism of the reform movement. Jonah himself ('The Dove'!) stands for the Israel of 400BC, unwilling to share its privileges with the pagan world outside ('Nineveh'), even when the exile gave them the perfect opportunity ('The Whale'). The author is revolted by the attitude which sees those outside the community of 'God's people' as an object only of God's punishment, and not of his mercy and love. Jesus was to make the same criticism of those who identified God with their own narrow ideas of him.

> *Why should I not be concerned for Nineveh?*
>
> *(Jonah 4:11)*

Zechariah 9-14

These chapters mark the end of the prophetical movement, a last attempt about 300BC to collect together and preserve from oblivion all the different themes preached by the great prophets of the past.

Being such a miscellany, the chapters are among the most obscure in the Old Testament. But the themes here preserved – of the Gathering of God's people into the true promised land, of the Coming of the king of peace, of the Return of God as shepherd of his people, of Paradise regained, of the Transformation of God's people into a race of priests dedicated to his worship – all these will be resumed in the New Testament, where they are seen as fulfilled in Jesus.

> *They will mourn for the one whom they have pierced*
> *as though for an only child.*
>
> *(Zechariah 12:10)*

Things to do . . .

Look up the following texts:

> *2 Samuel 7:1-7*
> *1 Kings 8:27*
> *Jeremiah 7:1-15*
> *Ezekiel 11 and 12*
> *Isaiah 66:1-2*
> *John 2:13-22*
> *Acts 6:13-14, 7:4-60, 17:24*

They all question whether God is best worshipped in a building. What are the advantages of having holy buildings? What are the drawbacks? Discuss.

Find some modern photographs (from newspapers, colour supplements, or from your own collection) which would illustrate the verses from the prophets quoted in this section, or any other verses you may choose.

Samson

The story of Samson and his outwitting of the Philistines is proverbial. It had become so even for the Israelites, whose telling of this early James Bond story has all the characteristics of a piece of popular folklore, with a hero who is marked out from birth, and whose physique, charm and wit make him the idol of women, and the bane of his enemies. The traditional story in Judges 13-16 is one of many used by the author of the book to illustrate his religious message.

It is the least typical of all the stories. Samson is more of a one-man-resistance movement than a national leader like the other heroes. Yet the story illustrates so perfectly the book's theme of unfaithfulness leading to disaster that its historical value fades into insignificance. Samson stands for the nation itself, dedicated to the God of Sinai from birth, deriving all its strength from that dedication, in constant danger of dissipating its strength by flirting with other gods, and collapsing in ruin as soon as that source of strength, like Samson's dedicated long hair, is cut off.

David

David was the first (and almost the only) successful king of Israel. When Samuel had reluctantly given in to the popular demand for a king, and the first candidate Saul had so dismally failed to live up to expectations (see 1 Samuel 8-15), it looked as if this Israelite experiment in a new form of government would be stillborn. It was David who saved the new constitution by sheer force of character, and gave the Israelite monarchy an impetus which was to maintain it in existence for four hundred years.

David's origins are obscure, but immediately before his rise to prominence he had been working as a mercenary for the Philistines who ruled the country, while trying to escape the clutches of his unsuccessful predecessor in the kingship-experiment, Saul. Backed by his own army of seasoned troops, David waited patiently until Saul died. He then presented himself to the Israelite tribes as their natural leader. His own southern tribe of Judah ('the Jews') accepted him immediately, and the northerners shortly after. The year was 1000BC.

Aware of the need for a centralised rallying point, one of the first things that David did was to establish a capital — the first that the tribesmen ever had. He chose the citadel of Jerusalem, one of the few towns in the land with its own self-sufficient water supply. Given the traditional rivalry between northern and southern tribes, it was a shrewd choice. It lay in neutral territory between north and south, and was in fact so impregnable that none of the tribes had so far been able to claim it for themselves. The inhabitants boasted that it could be defended by blind cripples. David sent a troop of commandos through its underground water-system, and captured the city from the inside (2 Samuel 5).

David's Jerusalem became the centre of a newly emerging nation. Under his leadership, the Israelite tribes were strong enough to convince the rest of Palestine that resistance was useless. It had been the custom of the time to eliminate enemies by slaughtering them wholesale. Under David, they were invited to throw in their lot with Israel. They did so. Even the Philistines, masters of the land just a few years earlier, and a threat to the continued survival of the Israelite tribes, are only mentioned from David's time on as members of his personal bodyguard (2 Samuel 8:18). One of David's most loyal officers was another absorbed 'foreigner' – the Hittite Uriah (see 2 Samuel 11).

The nations surrounding this newly united people of Israel also felt the impact of David's reign. To the east, the Ammonite kingdom (whose modern capital is still called Amman) was subjected to direct rule from Jerusalem. The powerful kingdoms to the north (later known as Syria) and to the south (Moab and Edom) were made vassal states, paying tribute-money to David. To the west, a peace-treaty was signed with the independent seafaring Phoenicians on the Lebanese coast.

David therefore emerged as the head of a veritable empire. Not that he could ever be counted as a serious threat or rival to the powerful empires already long established in Egypt, Mesopotamia and Asia Minor. But it is an indication of his achievement that he put Israel on the contemporary map of the world.

Defended by cripples.

© Juliette John

The portrait of David given in the Bible is probably (like the later traditional English portrait of king Arthur) idealised. He was no saint. There were elements of the military dictator about him. He knew when to seize the main chance and, in the spirit of the times, did not hesitate to use violence to reach his ambition.

Yet his achievement cannot be denied. When the story of the events that led up to his time came to be written, it was designed to point to David as its climax. And all those who wrote of the events subsequent to David are clearly yearning in their heart for 'another David'. When the first Christians, a thousand years later, wanted to express what Jesus of Nazareth meant to them, that is the title they gave him.

Solomon and the Temple

The choice of Jerusalem as a capital was not only a political act. One of David's shrewdest moves was to bring to the new capital the portable chest known as the ark of the covenant, dating from the nomadic past history of the tribes. It contained the two stone tablets on which were inscribed their God-given laws, and so was a symbol of the covenant which bound them to God. By making Jerusalem the resting place of this ark, David ensured that from now on the king should be the custodian of the nation's religious traditions.

It comes as no surprise, therefore, that the story of David's successor, Solomon, revolves around the account of his building of the permanent shrine to house the ark – the temple.

The temple stood on Jerusalem's highest point, 'nearest' to heaven. The ark was housed in a windowless room, flanked by two gigantic gilded and winged creatures. These provided the throne of God. The dark empty space above them symbolised his mysterious presence. No one was allowed to enter this Holy of Holies except the high priest, and he only once a year. This shrine gave on to the main temple building, and eventually on to a porch which led out into a spacious colonnaded courtyard. Here the congregation gathered around the stepped altar of sacrifice, itself a small mountain.

The temple was not without its critics, even though it was designed first and foremost as the 'chapel royal' for the adjoining palace. Yet because it housed the ark of the covenant, it gradually displaced the places of worship which had been set up elsewhere, and became the embodiment of the nation's religion, and the symbol of its identity.

The story of the temple (and its adjoining palace) occupies a central position in the biblical account of Solomon's reign. The project eventually cost him his throne. To meet the high costs involved, he had to impose heavy taxes on his people, submit them to forced labour, and even mortgage a part of his northern territories. This aroused so much opposition that his successor Rehoboam faced the immediate rebellion of half his population, who set up an independent kingdom in the north, and called themselves 'Israel'. Judah in the south, this suggested, had now forfeited that title.

In the light of these final events, it is difficult to judge whether Solomon's reign should be counted as a success or a failure. Some would see Solomon only as David's prodigal son, frittering away his father's hard-won kingdom. This is the judgement of the biblical account, which has nothing but praise for David and, in its closing pages, little but condemnation for Solomon. But it is important to appreciate that this judgement is based on later religious considerations. Others would be more sympathetic to Solomon, and see him as a pioneer who courageously tried to lead his timorous people out of their isolation into the real world of their time. If he failed, it was because his people were not ready for such a venture of faith.

His achievements were not small. In a time of considerable turmoil, he gave his people forty years of peace. In place of his father's expansionist policy, which had required the constant use of force, he maintained a happy relationship with the neighbouring nations by diplomatic means. The legendary expression 'Solomon and his thousand wives' was a tribute, not to his sex life, but to his diplomacy – he formed political alliances with his neighbours by the recognised expedient of including their princesses in his harem.

Far from destroying David's work, therefore, Solomon seems to have consolidated it with extraordinary ability. His building projects turned Jerusalem from a village into an international capital. The commercial flair with which he made Israel a market place for the whole Middle East gave his people a standing they have never since surpassed. In terms of commerce, culture and prosperity, the reign of Solomon was Israel's Golden Age.

Perhaps Solomon's greatest achievement, and certainly the most lasting, was literary. In our age of universal education, we find it difficult to imagine a time when anything needing to be written or read required the services of a specialist – the scribe. Solomon's complex

© UNRWA, G. Nehmen

activities required the recruitment and training of a whole army of scribes. They were needed to make accounts, to record taxes and receipts, to draw up administrative lists, to conduct international correspondence, and to transcribe treaties. As the temple liturgy grew, a permanent record needed to be kept of the prayers and hymns used there.

Most important of all, Solomon initiated the task of putting into writing the folklore, sagas, songs, myths and historical memories which made up the traditions of the tribes that called themselves Israel, and which so far had been handed down by word of mouth. The work of collecting this material, and co-ordinating it into a single narrative which would stand as an expression of the nation's identity and faith – this far outlasted Solomon. It even outlasted his dynasty, because it is the basis of the book venerated by Jews and Christians as their Bible.

It is no wonder that 'the wisdom of Solomon' became legendary. He was regarded as sharing in God's own wisdom, and all the later Wisdom literature was dedicated to his name. This gives point to the New Testament's description of Jesus as 'something greater than Solomon' (Matthew 12:42), someone in whom the wisdom of God had become flesh and blood (1 Corinthians 1:24).

It fell to Elisha to complete Elijah's task. Inheriting his master's spirit, he continued to fight against the encroaching Baal-religion, and engineered the blood-bath which this primitive age regarded as necessary to replace a corrupt dynasty and save the true religion. Like his master before him, he was acclaimed as 'The Chariots of Israel and its Horsemen' (2 Kings 2:12, 13:14). Each in their turn, they were worth a whole army to their people.

It is no longer possible to assess the historical value of many of the Elijah and Elisha stories. The author of the books of Kings has clearly incorporated them as they already existed, amplified and embroidered by oral tradition, as is the way with popular Lives of the Saints. That both of them were healers may safely be presumed. But their real importance lies in the impetus they gave to the prophetical movement, and in their championship of the God who was so often betrayed by the Israelite kings. Without their work there would have been no Amos, Hosea, Isaiah and Jeremiah to press home the implications of the covenant made at mount Sinai. In Israelite tradition, Elijah was said never to have really died. A cup of wine and an empty chair is kept for him at every Passover celebration, where his return is still awaited. The tradition underlines the veneration in which he has always been held.

In the New Testament, Elijah figures frequently as a summary of the whole prophetical movement, and its promise of the new covenant which God would make with his people. It announces that, in the person of John the Baptist, Elijah had as it were returned to complete the work he had begun (see Matthew 17:1-13).

Elijah and Elisha

To the casual reader, the books of Kings present little more than an interminable list of the successors of David and Solomon who, almost without exception, 'did what is displeasing to Yahweh'. With a sigh of relief the reader welcomes the break in the dreary narrative provided by the vivid stories of Elijah and Elisha in 1 Kings 17 – 2 Kings 13.

The ninth century BC was a critical time in Israel's history. Divided into two kingdoms at Solomon's death, the nation was no longer strong enough to withstand the onslaught of its enemies, both material and spiritual. In the northern kingdom particularly, an alliance with Phoenicia almost saw the end of any recognition of the God who had rescued this people from Egypt and brought them to the promised Land. Under queen Jezebel, their God Yahweh was first confused with, and then replaced by, the Phoenician god Baal.

It was this crisis that was met by Elijah. His name was already an eloquent protest in itself: in Hebrew, *Elijahu* means 'Yahweh alone is God'. King Ahab called him 'The Troubler of Israel'. The famous challenge he issued on mount Carmel (see 1 Kings 18) would be remembered for all time as proof that Yahweh alone could give blessing and fruitfulness to his people, and that Baal was no god at all. And the lonely journey he made to mount Horeb (Sinai) (1 Kings 19) would remind Israel for all time where its faith was rooted.

Immanuel

The Hebrew word *immanu-El* means 'God is with us'. It is the name given by Isaiah to the mysterious child who, he promises, will deliver God's people from their enemies and inaugurate a reign of peace. The promise was made to king Ahaz at a time when the Davidic dynasty was threatened with extinction. The birth of the child was to be a guarantee to the king that in spite of all appearances, God was standing firm by his promise to 'be with' the House of David for all time. The chapters in which Isaiah enthusiastically describes the blessings that this royal child will bring (7-12) have been given the title 'The Book of Immanuel'.

The references throughout these chapters are not to a remote future, but to events connected with the threatened invasion of Palestine by Syria and Assyria between the years 730 and 700BC. This makes it probable that 'the virgin' from whom Immanuel was to be born refers to Israel itself, frequently described by the prophets as the virgin bride of God. Micah, a contemporary of Isaiah, also looks forward to a deliverer born to the virgin Zion in the midst of her travails (see Micah 4:6 – 5:5). It was in fact Ahaz's successor Hezekiah who safeguarded the continuation of the royal line in Jerusalem, and who, by rejecting foreign alliances and relying on God alone, brought peace to his people when the neighbouring nations were deported.

None of Hezekiah's own successors lived up to the high hopes Isaiah had placed in him. In fact the whole royal line was finally extinguished soon after. Yet texts like Isaiah 7-12 continued to be read and prayed in the hope that they would eventually find a deeper fulfilment. The New Testament picks up that hope. It opens with a summary of Old Testament history that culminates in Mary, who is seen as the perfection of Israel, the ideal bride of God. It was her son Jesus, says Matthew, who is the true Immanuel, in whom God is close to his people for all time (see Matthew 1:23 and 28:20).

© UNRWA, M. Nasr

The Suffering Servant

The four Songs of the Suffering Servant form part of the Book of Consolation (Isaiah 40-55) written during the Babylonian exile of the sixth century BC. They are arranged to form a gradual climax, so that the Servant, whose commission is merely outlined in the first song (42:1-7), has by the second song (49:1-7) grasped something of the misunderstanding and suffering that this will entail. In the third song (50:4-10) he accepts his persecution, trusting blindly in God to vindicate him in the end. By the time we come to the last song (52:13 – 53:12) his suffering has become the main theme, with the realisation that his mission is to be fulfilled, not in spite of it, but because of it. His death is an act of self-sacrifice through which he wins the conversion of a thoughtless world and his own restoration to life.

The prophet sees this song as the expression of an ideal. This is the shape into which God has been trying to form Israel through the ages. This is an Israel which has outgrown its earlier dreams of national aggrandisement, and has been taught by its suffering an intimacy with God which it could never learn in its years of prosperity. This is an Israel, therefore, which achieves not only its own salvation, but also its vocation to be a channel of revelation and redemption to the world. Such an Israel has learnt to save its brethren and the whole world at the cost of itself.

The deep insight shown in these poems probably forms the culmination of Old Testament thought. It has not come to the prophet out of the blue. The outlines of his picture have already been traced in the great figures of the past – in the Joseph whose sufferings won the salvation of his brothers, in the David who had twice to pass through the testing ground of the desert before he could claim the kingdom, in the Jeremiah whose passionate love of his countrymen was only understood after they had made away with him, and in the innocent sufferer whose voice is heard in so many psalms. The clearest outline of the picture was being traced at the moment of writing by Israel itself, which is regularly given the title of Servant in the adjoining pages. In Babylonian exile the whole nation was beginning to learn the spiritual value of its suffering. Its patient resignation was not only bringing the knowledge of Yahweh to the outside world, but also beginning to move that world to acknowledge its own guilt.

The powerful portrait, then, is based on past and present reality. Yet it remains an ideal, preached to rather than merely applied to the exiles in Babylon. Strangely, there is almost no reference back to this ideal in subsequent Old Testament writings. It is not until the Gospels came to be written that the theme of the Suffering Servant is taken up again, to be applied to Jesus of Nazareth.

It is probable that Jesus based his own life and teaching on these pages: the temptation story with which his ministry begins is a symbol of his refusal to accept anything other than the way of the cross. Certainly it is to these pages that his first followers referred again and again, as they tried to explain the meaning of the death of Jesus, the Jew in whom the genius of Israel had found its fullest expression, the embodiment of an ever suffering Israel.

See		
	Matthew 8:17	*The Bearer of our sickness*
	Matthew 12:17	*The silent Servant*
	Mark 10:45	*The Servant who gives his life as ransom*
	Luke 24:26	*The Messiah who must suffer*
	John 12:38	*The rejected Servant*
	Acts 3:13-26	*The glorified Servant*
	Acts 8:32	*The Lamb for slaughter (= John 1:29?)*
	Romans 4:25	*Handed over to death*
	Philippians 2:7	*The Slave who accepts death*
	1 Peter 2:24	*The Healer of our wounds*

C. The Writings

Everything written about me,
in the Law of Moses,
in the Prophets,
and in the Psalms,
was destined to be fulfilled.

(Luke 24:44)

© Barnaby's Picture Library

The risen Christ's last instructions to his apostles, according to Luke, is a demonstration of how his life and death had been a fulfilment of the whole Old Testament. Luke divides it, as Jews have always done, into three. We have looked at the first two sections. The third is here referred to as The Psalms, although psalms only form part of this final Old Testament section, The Writings.

Under this title have been collected twenty books, many of which might easily have been incorporated in the sections already analysed above. But those sections had already been finalised and accepted as sacred Scripture. These twenty books were all written or finished later, and still had to prove their worth. Indeed some were written so late that they never made the grade among the Jews in Palestine, and so came to be called 'deuterocanonical' (see above page 22). Inevitably such a collection is a disorderly miscellany. For convenience, they have been grouped here in as logical a sequence as possible, to highlight what few connections exist between them.

1. A Book of Prayers

Many of the prayers we use are prayers of petition or asking. Most of the prayers included in the **Book of Psalms** are prayers of praise. In fact the Hebrew name for them is *Tehillim*, 'The Praises'.

Praising God is one of the most fundamental of human needs. When a Russian Orthodox believer was recently asked what was the most important moment of the liturgy, he replied without hesitation: 'When all the faithful praise God in the hymn of the cherubim, "Holy, holy, holy".' For him, that was even more important than receiving the Eucharist. The 'Praises' express perfectly this human longing to praise God. The Psalms are a collection of hymns in which Israel sings to God of its joy, its sorrow, and especially its praise.

As religious songs, the psalms have no equal in the literature of any age or country. This is due not only to the sincerity and dignity with which they speak of God and his relationship with humans, but to the fact that believers have accepted them as inspired prayer. For them, these are the words which God, like a father teaching his children to speak his name, has placed on the lips of his chosen people, so that they should know how to sing his glory and implore his blessing as they make their way towards him.

Every human mood is expressed in these prayers, from fear to confidence, from anxiety and frustration to peace and radiant happiness, from a sense of the slavery of sin to a sense of joy in the freedom of God. War songs are here, and songs of peace-time. There are prayers of personal suffering, and prayers of national emergency.

The name of David has traditionally been associated with the psalter. No doubt it was he who taught his people to pray to God about their joys and sufferings and hopes in this simple and moving way. It may well be that he himself composed some of the songs in this book. What is certain is that his collection was added to after his death. Even psalms that he may himself have composed would later have been adapted to fit new circumstances and needs. The result is that it is no longer possible to give a precise date to many of the psalms. As we have received them, they reflect not just one age, but the whole history of Israel. The titles at the head of many of them, often poorly translated in older versions of the Bible, usually indicate the later liturgical usage of the psalms, and are not a safe guide as to their origin.

Having been the songs of the Jewish temple and synagogue, the psalms naturally became the songs of the Christian Church which sprang from them. Jesus himself had prayed these words from childhood, and used them in worship throughout his life. His preaching is punctuated with quotations from the psalms, and it was the psalms that gave him his dying words.

2. Six Philosophical Books

All peoples venerate their philosophers or wise men. All cultures have their store of 'wisdom' or collection of wise sayings, maxims which summarise the experience of past generations, and so give people guidance in the widest sense.

In the east, it was around the king especially that a caste of 'wise men' grew up, as a sort of civil service to help him administer his kingdom. As such, the collection of advice they passed on from one generation to the other ('My son, listen to the word of your father . . . ') was entirely functional, and had no particular religious purpose.

But in Israel, the monarchy was not an absolute one. It was deeply influenced by the prophets, who insisted that the king was only a human representative of the true King, God. This view was imposed on the 'wise men' too: their wisdom was valid only if it reflected the true wisdom of God. The beginning and foundation of all true wisdom was the 'fear' or reverent worship of the Lord. Wisdom was ultimately identified with virtue, and folly with sin.

When the monarchy collapsed in the sixth century BC, Israel put all its future hopes in this true wisdom, and even began to attribute to this wisdom the qualities once associated with the hoped-for Second David. It is no exaggeration to say that this search for true wisdom gave birth to the most important development of Jewish thought in the last five hundred years before Christ.

An optimistic school continued to repeat the traditional view that happiness could only come from the practice of virtue. Sin could only lead to disaster. A more pessimistic school criticised this glib solution. It might in the long run be true on a national scale, but at the individual level the fact is that saints often suffer and sinners go scot free. Both schools yearned for God's inscrutable wisdom to be made manifest on earth. The New Testament will claim that Jesus was the answer to this prayer.

The Optimists

Since 'wisdom' was associated so closely with the monarchy, Israel's traditions spoke of its most illustrious king, Solomon, as the greatest wise man of all time. All its Wisdom literature was placed under his patronage and name, as all Law was placed under the name of Moses, to indicate that his spirit continued in it.

The book of **Proverbs**, the oldest of Israel's collections of wise sayings, explicitly attributes two large groups of these sayings to Solomon (see 10:1 and 25:1). But other groups are associated with other wise men (see 22:17, 24:23, 30:1, 31:1), and the final collection was not put together in the present form until about 500BC, when the prophets had already exercised a profound spiritual influence on Israel's thought. This explains why, amid the many examples of purely secular wisdom, the conviction is frequently expressed that true wisdom comes only from God. In fact the whole book is prefaced with nine chapters exhorting the reader to strive after such true wisdom.

In its general tendency, Proverbs represents the more optimistic solution to the problems which faced Israel's wise men: wisdom (virtue) is rewarded by God with happiness; all unhappiness comes from its opposite, sin.

The deutero-canonical book of **Ecclesiasticus** belongs to the same school of thought, though it was compiled much later, perhaps about 200BC. A vast manual of advice and piety, it comprises several collections of wise sayings, each preceded by a poem in praise of the wisdom which God has revealed to his people. It is addressed to the author's many contemporaries, who were tempted to abandon the Jewish way of life for a Greek one. Along with a number of other books written about this time, it was not universally regarded as part of Scripture, but accepted as profitable for 'ecclesiastical' reading. This was the most popular of such books. Hence its title.

© Andes Press Agency

From about the same time, and the same school of thought, comes the deutero-canonical book of **Tobit**. It is the story of a pious Israelite who is subjected to the most trying circumstances, but who remains faithful to God throughout, confident in God's help and reward. His anguish is matched only by that of Sarah, another innocent person suffering unjustly, and turning to God for an answer. Their prayers do not go unanswered. God's providence becomes concrete in the person of the angel Raphael, who brings to both the reward for their loyalty.

The book seems to be telling a history. In fact the story whatever its value as history, is simply a vehicle for the writer to convey his conviction that suffering must be seen simply as a test of sincerity, sent by a God who is hiddenly but constantly present in the suffering, who hears the cry for help, and who will ultimately reward those who remain faithful. The solution is inadequate, as other Wisdom books will point out. But no solution can afford to reject this fundamental conviction.

The Pessimists

The story of **Job** has become proverbial. A wise pagan of patriarchal times, rich and happy beyond all description, has his possessions, his family and even his health taken away from him as a test of his faithfulness to God. His 'comforters' only add to his distress by their suggestion that this is a punishment for his own wickedness. His patient fidelity to God is finally rewarded when everything is restored to him twofold.

The story was already proverbial (see Ezekiel 14:14-20) when the present book of Job came to be written about 500BC. Its author has simply split it into two, and used it as a prose framework (chapters 1-2 and 42) for his own criticism of the story, in some of the finest poetical passages of the Bible. Under the form of a dialogue between Job and his three friends (giving Job nine innings), the various traditional solutions to the problem of suffering are discussed – punishment for the sins of his youth, of his unconscious, of his ancestors, of his children. One by one they are rejected as irrelevant to this case, and in any case unworthy of God.

No alternative solution is offered. Even God's intervention at the end only emphasises the fact that to the limited human mind the suffering of the innocent must always remain a mystery. But the book has shown that to clear away inadequate solutions does not weaken faith, but only strengthens it, the true faith that serves God not for reward but for himself alone.

The word **Ecclesiastes** means 'The Preacher (of wisdom)'. Under the accepted literary fiction referred to above, the anonymous writer of the book assumes the mantle of the great wise man Solomon in order to incorporate his work into Israel's Wisdom literature.

In fact, though he writes 300 years later, about 200BC, he belongs to the same school of thought as the author of Job, and writes in order to criticise the comfortable doctrine that wisdom and virtue necessarily lead to happiness. In a series of realistic meditations, the author comes to the repeated conclusion that everything we can experience is 'vanity', that is to say empty, unsubstantial, unable to satisfy our infinite appetite for happiness. We cannot give our whole heart to anything ('a time for giving birth') because it is always threatened by its opposite ('a time for dying' – in the much quoted chapter 3). Not without humour and humility, the author advises his readers to be thankful for the small consolations this life nevertheless offers.

The author has gone deeper even than the book of Job. Suffering is not the problem. Even a life without suffering is futile, transitory and unsatisfying. He offers no positive solution to the problem. But in emphasising the inadequacy of all worldly reward, he has pointed to the need for a deeper answer. The New Testament will claim to give such an answer.

© Barnaby's Picture Library

The Breakthrough?

The last of Israel's Wisdom books, written as late as 100 or 50BC, calls itself quite baldly **Wisdom**. It suggests that previous attempts to solve the problem of evil had always been unsuccessful because life and death were thought of in terms of 'persons', and when persons die, that is the end.

But if persons are thought of in terms of 'souls' inside 'bodies', then there could be a breakthrough. The union with God which is brought about by true wisdom (virtue) is something which death cannot break, for though the body may die, the soul is immortal. It is this wisdom, possessed by Israel alone, which the author, another 'Solomon', recommends to those of his countrymen who are beginning to adopt the new Greek philosophy.

Yet in doing so, he has himself had to adopt a Greek mind. No Hebrew mind was able to tolerate for long this strange Greek dichotomy between soul and body. What Jews continued to long for was a resurrection of the whole person, not simply an immortality of 'the soul'.

3. Echoes of Jeremiah

Two short books among The Writings are associated with the name of the great prophet Jeremiah, and in some Bibles these are printed alongside his preaching. **Lamentations** seems in fact to have been written shortly after his time, to mourn the destruction of Jerusalem in 586BC. Its five poems are in alphabetical form, each verse beginning with a new letter of the Hebrew alphabet, like some of the psalms. Based on Jeremiah's own passionate love for Jerusalem, the poems were composed for liturgical use on the site of the ruined temple, an annual fast day on which the book is still chanted by Jews today.

The name of Jeremiah's secretary **Baruch** has been used to give some unity to a miscellany of short passages on repentance, the Law as divine wisdom, the return from exile, and idolatry. Some pieces may be quite ancient, but they were only edited about 50BC outside Palestine, among the Jewish communities who tried to put the exiled Jeremiah's ideals into practice. They are therefore fittingly connected with his name.

4. Three Religious Histories

About 450BC, someone decided that alongside the Deuteronomic History that already existed (Joshua-Judges-Samuel-Kings, see above page 31), Israel needed another. His work comprises the books of **1 Chronicles-2 Chronicles-Ezra-Nehemiah**.

Chronicles has in some versions been called Paralipomenon, a word which means 'leftovers'. It is an unfortunate title, since it suggests that it is nothing more than a supplement to the books of Samuel and Kings. It is in fact a completely fresh look at the history of the kings of Israel, in the light of the new priestly spirituality which grew up among the Jews in the Babylonian exile. This spirituality, the same as that which had produced the book of Leviticus (see above page 24), had abandoned all further political hopes, and concentrated on making the small Jewish community which returned from exile into a Church, intent only on the worship of the Holy One who dwelt in their midst.

The past is seen largely as a failure to live up to this ideal, and past stories – the same as those used by the books Samuel and Kings – are adapted to press home the point. Modern historians might be shocked to find that Solomon's payment of twenty Galilee towns to the king of Tyre in 1 Kings 9:11 becomes a gift in reverse direction in 2 Chronicles 8:2, or that David's payment of fifty silver shekels for the temple site in 2 Samuel 24:20 grows into six hundred gold shekels in 1 Chronicles 21:22. But the stories here, as indeed anywhere else in the Bible, are never told as straight history, only as illustrations of a theological message.

This religious interpretation of history does not stop, as the Deuteronomic History did, at the exile. It is brought up to date by the addition of the memoirs and official documents in which the return from exile is seen as a sign of God's faithfulness, and an appeal to Judaism to respond in kind. The memoirs are those of Ezra and Nehemiah, the two great reformers, who strove to make the priestly ideal a reality.

The narrow exclusivism of some of their measures, especially against the Samaritans drew protest from other writers (see Jonah page 37 and Ruth page 46). But in the crisis of the time their work succeeded in making God's people a People Apart, dedicated to the Law, and longing for the Messiah. It was Jews of this kind that became the first disciples of Jesus.

An even greater crisis faced the Jews when they came under Greek rule in the second century BC, and faced the persecution of the Greek emperor Antiochus Epiphanes. Forbidden under pain of death to practise their religion, many apostasised. A few, with tremendous faith and against overwhelming odds, were determined to fight for conscience sake. They won.

1 Maccabees is a fairly straightforward chronicle of this resistance movement from 175 to 135BC. Its first leader Judas, who gave his nickname *Maqqaba* or 'Hammer' to the

© Eastern Counties Newspapers

whole movement, recaptured Jerusalem in 164BC and restored the desecrated temple to his people. The book greets him with enthusiasm:

> He extended the fame of his people.
> Like a giant, he put on the breastplate . . .
> he engaged in battle after battle,
> protecting the ranks with his sword.
> He was like a lion in his exploits . . .
> his memory is blessed for ever and ever . . .
> His name resounded to the ends of the earth,
> he rallied those who were on the point of perishing.
> *(1 Maccabees 3:1-9)*

His efforts were crowned with success when Judah regained complete political independence under the leadership of his brothers Jonathan and Simon.

2 Maccabees is not a sequel, nor even strictly speaking a history. Its author has chosen out some of the more colourful popular traditions about the early days of the war, in order to emphasise God's protection of the Jerusalem temple. He also stresses the faith of the martyrs who died for this cause. They had arrived at the conclusion, perhaps for the first time in the Old Testament, that their death would not cheat them of victory. God would raise them up again, bodies as well as 'souls', to enjoy the glory of his Kingdom.

Both books of Maccabees are deutero-canonical (see above page 22), and were written shortly before 100BC.

5. Three Parables

Parables have always been used, especially in the east, as a dramatic way of teaching religion. Jesus himself made use of them frequently. We ought not to be surprised to find them in the Old Testament, even expanded as in the case of these three works into complete books. It is no longer possible to tell how far, if at all, the stories are based on actual fact. Nor does this matter, since it is not for their historical content that they were told, any more than Jesus' stories were.

The book of **Ruth** is one of the most charming in the Old Testament. It tells of the devotion of a foreign girl to her Jewish mother-in-law, and of a sense of duty far outshining anything shown by her Israelite contemporaries. Through her marriage to Boaz, she becomes the great-grandmother of king David. Hence the position of the book in our western Bibles.

It seems in fact to have been written at the same time as the book of Jonah, about 400BC, as a protest against the narrowness of the reforms which at that time wished to exclude foreigners like the Samaritans (see below on this page) from the Jewish community. As such, its teaching is the same as that of Jesus' story of the Good Samaritan.

The books of **Judith** and **Esther** both tell of the deliverance of God's people at the hands of a woman from a destruction which, humanly speaking, seemed inevitable. They contain details taken from every period in Israelite history – Assyrian, Babylonian and Persian – in order to suggest that there is never a time in which God will not come to the help of his people if they remain faithful.

The language they use indicates that the books were written as late as the second century BC, when the apostasy of many Jews under the persecution of the Greek empire made that lesson urgently important. This urgency, while it does not excuse, at least explains the ferocity of both books. The two heroines stand for the whole of Judaism (the name Judith actually means 'Jewess') face to face with paganism, putting all its beauty and intelligence into the hands of God to win the victory.

6. An Apocalypse

The book of **Daniel** cannot be understood without some knowledge of the background against which it was written. It seems to be telling us about what went on in the Babylonian exile in the sixth century BC. In fact, both its position in the Hebrew Bible and its precise detail about Maccabean times indicate it was written much later, about 165BC, to give encouragement and hope to the Maccabees in their struggle against the almost successful Greek attempt to obliterate Judaism.

The stories of the King's Dream, the Golden Statue, Nebuchadnezzar's Madness, Belshazzar's Feast, Daniel in the Lion's Den, Susanna, Bel and the Dragon – these would be seen by outsiders simply as harmless tales of the olden days. In fact, the characters in these stories, just like those in the books of Esther and Judith, are only a thin disguise for the heroes of the resistance movement, and serve to express the author's conviction that God will not allow his faithful ones to see corruption. And Daniel's visions (chapters 7-12) serve the same purpose. Here the 'prophetical' style of direct exhortation and preaching has given way to the more dramatic 'apocalyptic' style.

'Apocalypse' is the successor of prophetism. When prophets ceased about 300BC, their apparently unfulfilled prophecies about the Day of the Lord needed to be repeated in more dramatic form. Past history would be shown, not as humans see it stretching backwards, but as God sees it stretching forwards, determined, guided, and directed towards his final victory. So an imaginary stance in the past is taken up, where God grants his friends visions of 'the future', always concluding on God's victory. Readers will appreciate the accuracy of the visions up to the present. Can they doubt the finale, God's ultimate triumph?

Daniel's 'visions' constitute a highpoint in Old Testament spirituality. Salvation is here seen as something that cannot be achieved by human means. God must himself intervene and bestow his Kingdom on the humane 'Man' who will replace the 'Beasts' that have so far ruled the world (Daniel 7:27). This text will have a profound influence on the New Testament (see Son of Man below, page 53).

Samaritans

Samaria was the town chosen by king Omri as a capital for the northern tribes of Israel after they had seceded from Judah to set up an independent kingdom (1 Kings 16:24). From this time until the city's destruction by the Assyrians in 721BC, the Old Testament uses the name to denote the whole of the northern kingdom of Israel, just as 'Jerusalem' epitomises the southern kingdom of Judah.

To replace its exiled inhabitants, Assyria colonised Samaria with a variety of displaced persons from other conquered territories (2 Kings 17). The intermarriage of these with the remaining Israelites seems to have produced a mongrel race known as the Samaritans, whom the Jewish exiles later returning from Babylonia no longer recognised as brothers, even though they remained faithful to the worship of Yahweh, and the observance of the Law of Moses.

In the fifth century BC, they offered to help the Jews rebuild the ruined Jerusalem temple. They were rebuffed by the chauvinist reformers Ezra and Nehemiah, and forced to erect their own on a high place even more venerable than Jerusalem – mount Gerizim – where they continue to this day to celebrate their annual Passover with great solemnity in the Moses tradition. For the Jews, this act set the seal on the schism between the two nations, and they have remained estranged ever since.

Jesus' attitude was less adamant. While he acknowledged his own Jewish nation's prior claim on him (Matthew 10:5), he yet recognised the close relationship of the Samaritans to his own people, and did not hesitate to present his message of salvation to them (see John 4, Luke 17:16). He even made a Samaritan the hero of one of his stories (Luke 10:33), and his resurrection message to his disciple was to make Samaria the first stage of their proclamation of the Gospel to the wide world beyond (see Acts 1:8, 8:5, 9:31).

7. A Love Song

Song of Songs means 'The loveliest of all songs'. Because of its use of the name Solomon in chapter 3, some Bibles place this book among the philosophical writings analysed above. But in fact it shows no interest in the problems discussed in those books. It is simply a series of poems about a lover's desire and search for his beloved, and about their delight in each other. The poetry is both brilliant and powerful. The language suggests it was written some time after 400BC, perhaps as late as 200BC.

Though some have always objected, these poems have from the beginning been taken by many quite literally, as a straightforward celebration of human love. And why should such a noble theme not form part of God's word to the human race?

In this interpretation, the different scenes here enacted are simply symbols of Old Testament history – of God's wooing of Israel in the Sinai desert (chapter 1), of his bringing her to his home in Palestine (chapter 2), of their union in the temple of Solomon (chapters 3-4), of Israel losing him in the Babylonian exile (chapters 5-6), and of his leading her back to the second temple (chapters 7-8).

Such an interpretation may seem artificial. But allegory is of its nature artificial, and if the author intended to write an allegory, he could not avoid being artificial. Certainly there is a strong Christian tradition to read the book in this way. If this tradition has interpreted the author correctly, then the Song of Songs is a perfect summary of the Old Testament, as a divine love story.

© Barnaby's Picture Library

Things to do . . .

Using the repetitive Hebrew manner, compose a psalm of your own, to express praise, or thanksgiving, or intercession, or anger.

What proverbs do you know (or can make up) which express optimism or pessimism about life's problems?

Write a parable which might give encouragement to Christians in South Africa, or in Northern Ireland, or in a Third World country.

Others have seen this language of lovers as a bold figure of speech for the love between God and his people. Certainly it is a language which many of the prophets used to express the joy and intimacy of this relationship (see especially Hosea 1-3), and the figure of speech continues to be exploited throughout the Bible down to its last page (Revelation 21:2).

The New Testament

*C*hristians are surprised when they first discover that fellow Christians have bound into their Bibles a writing of their own, the Book of Mormon, and regard it as quite as much the word of God as the rest. Jews must have found it equally strange when fellow Jews, as followers of Jesus, added their own writings to the Jewish Bible, and claimed that they too were part of sacred Scripture. Yet the friends of Jesus were convinced that God's covenant with Israel, of which the 'Old Testament' had told, was only part of the story of God's plans. Through Jesus, they claimed, God had extended that covenant to the whole world. They called their writings the Renewed Covenant, or New Testament. This section analyses its 27 books.

Before we considered the individual books of the Old Testament, we looked at the headings under which they should be put, since headings influence the way in which books are approached and understood. We shall do the same for the books of the New Testament.

The contents page of most New Testaments divides the books into three groups: Historical Books (Gospels and Acts), Doctrinal Books (The Epistles), and Prophetical Book (Revelation). In actual fact the books fall more naturally and coherently into four groups, and it would seem best to approach them in this way:

A. The Good News

Three parallel attempts, based on much the same sources, to interpret the meaning of Jesus' life and death as the good news of God's salvation.

Mark
Matthew
Luke

B. The Pauline Books

The continuation of Luke's Gospel into a second volume, to provide a background for the work of Paul, and his correspondence with the Christian communities he founded.

Acts of the Apostles	Colossians
1 Thessalonians	Philemon
2 Thessalonians	Ephesians
1 Corinthians	1 Timothy
2 Corinthians	2 Timothy
Philippians	Titus
Galatians	Hebrews
Romans	

C. The General Epistles

Letters written by other early Christian leaders to the Church at large.

James
1 Peter
Jude
2 Peter

D. The Johannine Books

John and his school tell the good news of what Jesus has come to mean to those who have known him for a very long time.

John's Gospel
3 Epistles of John
Revelation

A. The Good News

'Good News' is modern English for the Anglo-Saxon word *god-spel*. This is the word with which our ancestors accurately translated the Greek word *evangelion*, which is what the first Christians called the books with which the New Testament now opens. The Gospels were not the earliest of the New Testament writings. Nonetheless the first Christians decided they deserved star billing because they present the essence of the New Testament, the heart of the matter, the Good News.

The authors of the Gospels gave them no title. Why did the early Christians call them *The Good News* rather than *The Acts of Jesus* (as with The Acts of the Apostles), or *The Memoirs of Jesus* (as with Xenophon's Memoirs of Socrates), or *The Life of Jesus* (as with Plutarch's Lives)?

Presumably because they did not see these books – as people in later times tended to – as straight news reports. They saw them as having a deeper purpose – to proclaim the good news that God's plans for the world had been brought to completion in the person of Jesus of Nazareth. Such a proclamation is no longer a mere piece of information about the past. It demands a response from the reader, a change of heart, which the New Testament calls 'conversion'.

This explains why there is more than one Gospel. A simple biography of Jesus could have been written by a single news reporter. But if several writers duplicate and repeat a large amount of the same material, they are presumably saying that they are not writing a mere memorandum, but a message which can be presented in many ways. They are not taking so many photographs of Jesus, but painting their own portraits and offering their own interpretations of Jesus. These different interpretations have all mercifully been preserved for us, so that we can choose which (for the time being) means most to us.

© Barnaby's Picture Library

The New Testament Books in Context

As for the Old Testament, it will be useful to have a chronological table of the New Testament books, not only for reference, but so that we can see them in the context in which they were written.

Books of the Bible	Events in Palestine	Events Outside	Date
			BC
	Birth of Jesus.	Augustus Emperor.	6
	Death of Herod the Great.		4
	Archelaus rules in Judaea.		
	Herod Antipas rules in Galilee.		AD
	Judaea under Roman rule.		6
		Tiberius Emperor.	14
	Pontius Pilate governor.		26
	John the Baptist.		
	Ministry of Jesus.		
	Death of Jesus.		30
	Conversion of Paul.		36
	Mission to Samaria.	Caligula Emperor.	37
	Herod Agrippa rules Judaea.	Claudius Emperor.	41
	Paul's first journey.		45
	Council of Jerusalem.		
First written records of Jesus	Paul's second journey.		49
James			
1 Thessalonians			50
2 Thessalonians			51
	Paul's third journey		53
	based on Ephesus.	Nero Emperor.	54
1 Corinthians			56
2 Corinthians			57
Philippians			
Galatians	Paul in Corinth.		
Romans			
	Paul in prison.		58
	Paul sent to Rome.		60
Colossians			
Philemon			
Ephesians?			
Mark		Persecution of Christians in Rome.	65
1 Peter		Martyrdom of Peter.	
1 Timothy			66
2 Timothy			
Titus			
	Jewish War of Independence.	Martyrdom of Paul.	67
Hebrews		Galba Emperor.	68
		Vespasian Emperor.	69
	Destruction of Jerusalem.		70
	Fall of Masada.		73
Matthew			75
Jude		Titus Emperor.	79
		Domitian Emperor.	81
Luke			85
Acts			
Revelation		Persecution of Christians.	95
John			
Epistles of John		Nerva Emperor.	96
2 Peter			

This means that we can no longer see Jesus directly with our own eyes, only through the eyes of the evangelists. Yet it must immediately be added that they all present a coherent and consistent picture of a Galilee builder who called himself the **Son of Man**; who for a few short years took Palestine by storm with his preaching; who told parable after **parable** to make the bold claim that in his preaching the longed-for **Kingdom of God** was here and now being established; who corroborated that preaching in a healing ministry which his contemporaries saw as nothing short of **miraculous**; whose popularity with the masses was felt as such a threat by the religious establishment of the time – the **Scribes, Pharisees** and **Sadducees** – that they manoeuvred the occupying Roman powers into sentencing him to death by crucifixion; whose presence among his followers, far from being brought to a dead end, was so enriched by that death that they claimed his story had only now begun; and who in this **resurrection** experience acclaimed him as the awaited **Messiah-Christ**, indeed the very **Son of God**.

Christian propaganda? Without a doubt. Those who told such a story were not neutral reporters but believers. But they were convinced that others could discover the truth of that Easter faith for themselves if they committed themselves to the Good News they were proclaiming.

More about the **Son of Man** on page 53; **Parables** on page 54; **Kingdom of God** on page 54; **Miracles** on page 55; **Scribes** on page 57; **Pharisees** on page 57; **Sadducees** on page 58; **Resurrection** on page 58; **Messiah-Christ** on page 59; **Son of God** on page 60.

Mark's Gospel

Most scholars who have analysed the first three Gospels now agree that Mark must be recognised as the first to be written. It contains only thirty verses which are not to be found in either Matthew or Luke, who seem to have used Mark as their main source. Furthermore Mark regularly presents both Jesus and the disciples in a far harsher light than Matthew and Luke could bear – they both tone his text down, which suggests they wrote later. The complex relationship of the three writings is known as the **Synoptic Problem**.

Mark has used a number of existing short stories about Jesus and strung them together, sometimes quite haphazardly (there is no attempt to be chronological), in order to present a vivid 'video' of a person who both enthralled his contemporaries, and mystified them. 'Who can this be?' is the recurring question throughout these pages.

Mark answers the question in his opening line. He is the very Son of God (1:1). But this title, so conveniently provided on the first page, is not uttered again by any human lips until the last page (15:39). Why? Because for Mark it is a title so full of mystery that it will be bowdlerised if it is used too glibly, or too soon. Only when we see Jesus on the cross will we understand what becoming a son of God entails in the kind of world we live in. Before that, we ought not to use the word. Even Jesus' disciples got it wrong, and showed themselves to have the devil's own understanding of Jesus (see 8:33). To be son of God is not to have a title bestowed, but to have a role to play, a task to perform.

The Gospel was designed to give comfort to the persecuted Christians of Rome about the year AD65. Mark wants to assure them that their martyrdom is only an echo of Jesus'. It is a severe and demanding document. Yet Mark has written in a style so breathless and brilliant (the memoirs of Peter, says an ancient tradition), that all those who followed him – Matthew, Luke and John – adopted the formula he invented, to present the meaning of Jesus through a series of stories. Mark can be hailed as the first Christian Dramatist.

Synoptic Problem

The Gospels of Matthew, Mark and Luke are generally known as the *Synoptics* (a Greek word for 'look-alike') because of their remarkable similarity to each other. While nine tenths of John's text has no parallel in any of these three, Matthew and Luke have only a quarter of the text proper to themselves, and Mark only one twelfth. Matthew, Mark and Luke are clearly closely interrelated.

The precise nature of this interrelationship is known as the Synoptic Problem. Why call it a problem? Why not see all three as dependent on the same collection of oral traditions? Because there are frequent passages in these Gospels, even long ones, which correspond word for word, and which must therefore depend on each other or on a common written source. Yet alongside these closely matching passages, there are others which show such differences that it can only be concluded that each evangelist felt free to exercise a good deal of independence. The relationship of the three is therefore complex and problematical. Which evangelist was borrowing from which?

There is an early tradition that Matthew was the original Gospel, and that the other two are dependent on him. It is possible that this tradition refers to an earlier edition of Matthew, now lost. It cannot refer to the text of Matthew as we now have it, which shows such dependence on Mark that it is clearly secondary. After long years of comparing the texts closely, most scholars today agree that, of the three Synoptics, Mark must be the original, and that it was independently used by both Matthew and Luke as one of their sources.

Since both Matthew and Luke have much material in common which they have not borrowed from Mark, it is also possible that there was a second source available to them. This has been named Q. It is an apt name. It stands for the German word *Quelle* meaning 'source'. But it also suggests something with a question mark: it remains a hypothesis.

The material in Matthew and Luke which can be attributed to neither Mark nor Q (for instance, their Infancy stories) was presumably taken from the independent sources they each had access to. These are known as M and L. The picture which finally emerges would look something like this:

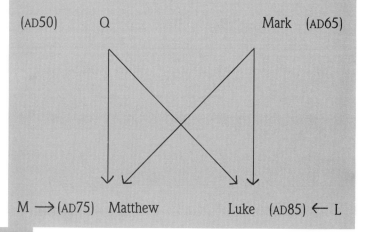

(AD50)   Q   Mark (AD65)

M → (AD75) Matthew   Luke (AD85) ← L

Matthew's Gospel

Since this Gospel is so heavily dependent on Mark (who was not a disciple of Jesus), it can safely be presumed that it was not written by one of the twelve close to Jesus. It has expanded Mark's material to twice the size by adding a number of long discourses representing the teaching of Jesus. It seems to have been composed about AD75 as an attempt to present a more elegant version of the Good News to the Greek world, in which Christianity was fast taking root.

Yet its elegance is Semitic rather than Greek. Jewish expressions and Jewish idioms are put into sentences with a Jewish repetitive pattern. Even the main body of the book is set out in the same rhythmical pattern, so that it falls into five parts, a new five-book Torah. Jesus appears as the New Moses, teaching the New Law. The very opening word of this Greek Gospel is 'Genesis'.

This New Law is announced in chapter 5 with the Sermon on the Mount, which opens with the challenging paradox of the **Beatitudes**. (More about the Beatitudes on page 61.) It is then developed in the other great discourses of chapters 10, 13, 18 and 24, each explaining the narrative that has gone before. Yet the Law of Jesus does not replace the Law of Moses. It brings it to perfection. The true Israel is now to be found, says Matthew, in the Christian community, whose members are assured on the first page that 'God is with us' (1:23), and on the last page that he will continue to be present with us till the end of time (28:20).

If Matthew's repetitive and rhythmical presentation lacks Mark's vitality, it has a tranquillity and dignity of its own. It is in this contemplative Semitic style that Jesus himself taught, and that the Christian liturgy continues to teach, because it echoes the rhythm of nature itself.

Luke's Gospel

'To go from Matthew to Luke', writes a recent commentator, 'is like coming out of the Church into the market-place'. The Christianity Luke presents is no longer a cause for martyrs to fight for (Mark), nor a Law for initiates to abide by (Matthew), but a message of common sense for all people. Luke is the first Humanist, whose writings take us right out of Palestine into a world the other evangelists don't dream of.

Where Mark's Gospel was too barbaric and Matthew's too Semitic, Luke's educated and orderly Greek approach was ideally suited for presenting the Gospel to the Greek world. Thorough as he is in his research (he has a quarter of his text proper to himself), tender in his interest, and universal in his outlook, it is Luke alone who tells us the

© UNRWA, J. Madvo

stories of Elizabeth, of Anna, of Jesus' women helpers, and of the widow of Nain. All the stories of Jesus' mother Mary come from Luke: she plays no part in Mark, and is totally silent in Matthew. Without Luke's Gospel we would never have heard of the prostitute who washed Jesus' feet, of the swindler Zacchaeus, of the repentant terrorist at Calvary, or of Jesus' last words of forgiveness. It is also Luke alone who records Jesus' parables of the Prodigal Father, of the Lost Sheep and the Lost Coin, of the Pharisee and the Publican, and of Dives and Lazarus. It is no surprise to find that Mark's recurrent phrase, 'They were afraid' has in Luke become, 'They rejoiced'.

Luke's Jesus, therefore, is no longer the Heroic Martyr of Mark, or the Majestic Teacher of Matthew, but the Universal Saviour, who comes to break down barriers, and who befriends above all the least and the lost. In this, his understanding of Jesus is close to that of Paul, whom he accompanied on some of his journeys. The Gospel seems to have been written between AD80 and 90.

Both Matthew and Luke have added an *'Infancy Gospel'* to the stories of Jesus they have in common with the other Gospels. For more on this see page 61.

Things to do . . .

'The Son of Man is Lord of the Sabbath'
'The son of man is lord of the sabbath'
Do the capital letters (the original had none) make any difference to the meaning?

List the ways in which the 'Kingdom of God' is something in the present. In what ways must we speak of it as something still in the future?

Try to list some of the 'miracles', greater than Jesus' own, which the disciples of Jesus have worked, as he promised.

To whom would you point as today's 'Scribes', 'Pharisees' and 'Sadducees'?

The difference between your group and a group of Jews could be simply expressed. You accept Jesus as Messiah-Christ, they don't. If the two groups met, what would they want to say to each other?

What do you find the most distinctive story told by Matthew, Mark and Luke? Why?

Take a section of the Gospel common to Mark, Matthew and Luke – say On Discipleship (Mark 10:13-22, Matthew 19:13-22, Luke 18:15-23), or The Storm at Sea (Mark 4:35-41, Matthew 8:18-27, Luke 8:22-25). Write out the text in three columns, a few words at a time, keeping the lines parallel, in the way two chapters of Mark are set out on page 14 above. Now compare the accounts meticulously, word by word, noting the slightest difference between the three. Do these say anything about the distinctive approach of the three evangelists?

Son of Man

The title 'son of man' occurs 86 times in the Gospels, and hardly at all in the rest of the New Testament. Since it always refers to Jesus, usually on his own lips, it seems to have been his characteristic way of talking about himself. In fact in some passages which are otherwise totally parallel, one text has him saying, 'The son of man', and the other simply, 'I'. Why did Jesus give himself that title? What did he mean?.

In Hebrew, 'son of' means 'belonging to the category of'. The 'sons of Shem' stands for all Semitic peoples. The 'sons of the prophets' refers to all who form part of the prophetical groups. When someone is called a son of man, therefore, it means basically no more than that he is a human being, someone belonging to the human race.

The prophet Ezekiel was particularly fond of the term, and applied it to himself no less than 93 times. In his case, he seemed to be emphasising man's essential fragility, weakness and distance from God – 'poor old Ezekiel' – a natural extension of his proper name, which means 'God is the strong one'.

Still with its basic meaning of 'man', the title takes on an entirely different shade of meaning in the book of Daniel. In one of the book's many visions, the successive Middle Eastern empires are described as so many nightmarish animals. These are finally superseded by a 'son of man' who ascends on the clouds to be crowned by God. The bestiality of Babylonia, Persia and Greece will be replaced by the humanity of the people of Israel. The identification is explicitly made in Daniel 7:27.

Later non biblical writers exploited this powerful imagery, and turned the 'son of man' metaphor into an actual heavenly person, pre-existent and otherworldly, scarcely distinct from God himself, descending from heaven on the clouds to establish the Kingdom of God, since it was becoming more and more evident that human forces alone could not bring it about. The 'son of man' had become the 'Son of Man', with a title paradoxically more divine than any 'son of God'.

So the various meanings of the term 'son of man' are clearly linked with each other, although they eventually became quite distinct from each other. Which of these meanings does the New Testament apply to Jesus? Strangely, all of them. In the different contexts in which Jesus is presented as 'son of man', he is in turn seen as a true member of the human race, as the weak and vulnerable victim, as the veritable embodiment of his people Israel, and as a divine visitant from heaven. Clearly some New Testament genius has seen the enormous possibilities lying within the ambiguous term 'son of man', and has fused them all together to apply them to Jesus.

Was this genius Jesus himself? Many feel compelled to say that it must have been. Others prefer to think that he himself used the term in an entirely neutral sense, meaning no more than 'I', and that it was his enthusiastic early disciples who gave the term the brilliant overtones it now carries in the Gospels.

Parables

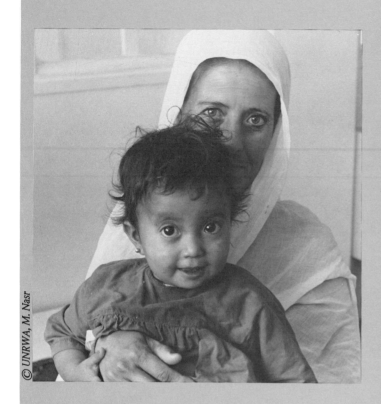

© UNRWA, M. Nasr

When Jesus' disciples asked him to explain the basic qualification for entering the Kingdom of God, he did not reply in abstract terms about humility, simplicity, sincerity and trustfulness. He simply grabbed a child and said, 'There it is' (see Matthew 18:2). He was teaching them by parable.

A parable is any story or action which conveys a truth in a concrete, vivid and pictorial manner. As such, it is a teaching aid in common use among all peoples. But it is so characteristic of the east that it affects the interpretation of the whole Bible. Throughout, it is the truth which the author is trying to convey that must be seized upon. The story itself, whether it is fiction, popular tradition or even a record of historical facts, exists only to illustrate this truth. Psalm 78:2, as we saw on page 31 above, calls a whole slice of Israel's history a 'parable'.

The psalm is quoted in Matthew 13:34 to characterise Jesus' preaching too. Skilled teacher that he was, he made it his normal practice to grasp his audience's attention and interest by speaking to them in concrete rather than abstract terms. The Gospel pages are filled with the stories he told for this purpose, and their vivid beauty has been the admiration of people throughout the ages. In spite of the difficult text of Mark 4:12, therefore, it would be ridiculous to suggest that Jesus actually used his parables to hide his teaching and mystify his hearers. If he had wanted to do that, he would have done better to say nothing at all.

Nevertheless the parables do not interpret themselves. Different readers have found vastly differing lessons in them. We need some clue if we are to seize the point they are making, and distinguish it from the many details which are only part of the supporting story. Jesus provided such a clue in speaking of many of them as 'parables of the Kingdom of God', and it is safe to presume that in his mind this was the purpose of all of them.

The parables of Jesus were designed to correct the mistaken notions of his contemporaries about the true nature of the Kingdom they were awaiting. This does not mean that they cannot be elaborated further to provide lessons for those who have found the Kingdom and try to live out its implications: the evangelists have in some cases clearly done so themselves (see Mark 4:13-20). But it does mean that to read them merely as general moral exhortations ('be good', 'be generous', 'be prudent') is to misunderstand them. They have a specific doctrinal purpose, to explain what God's Kingdom really is, and what it is not.

All the parables insist that the Kingdom is not some overwhelming cataclysm to come in the future, but something here and now present in the preaching of Jesus, demanding decision and commitment. Nor is it reserved for a chosen few. It is open to all, saints and sinners, who will abandon all to accept this priceless gift from God. All the parables are meant to shock, and turn people's ideas upside down. They all ask, 'Which character do you identify with?'

This means, of course, that the parables are essentially open-ended. In spite of what has been said above about their general purpose, none of them simply has *one* meaning. No story has. Jesus' usual conclusion is an invitation to his hearers to find their own meaning: 'Which of these . . . ?', 'What is your opinion?', 'Which of you . . . ?', 'What woman wouldn't . . . ?', 'Tell me what . . . ?'

Kingdom of God

The word 'kingdom' usually refers to the territory over which a king exercises his rule – the Kingdom of the Franks, the United Kingdom. The biblical phrase 'Kingdom of God' does not. It would be better translated 'King*ship* of God', because it refers primarily to God's rule over the universe which he created and continually keeps in being.

This authority or rule of God is an ever-present reality, but it became a hidden reality from the moment the human race attempted to set up an independent rule of its own. A central message of the Bible is that the day will come when it will again be openly manifested, when all people will again acknowledge God's universal Kingdom or rule, and live at peace in his presence.

This ideal was already partly achieved in the history of Israel. From its very birth at mount Sinai, Israel had been called to be a kingdom in which God manifested his presence (see Exodus 19:6). And when a human king was later chosen to govern the nation, it was only to make visible this invisible kingship of God. The Israelite kings ruled as God's representatives, and their task was to make the nations that did not yet know the true God acknowledge this. According to the biblical record, most of them failed dismally in this task, but the firm conviction remained that in the ideal future that dream would become a reality. Every failure was an invitation and an opportunity to renew that hope.

The New Testament does not break this line of thought, but continues it. It also points to the future for the full realisation of the Kingdom, when God's rule will be supreme. Jesus directs the attention of his disciples to that future day, comparing its joy to that of a wedding, or of a banquet, or of a family gathered round its father's table. The

© UNRWA

disciples themselves yearn for its coming with such urgency that in their writings they see the kingdoms of this world already in their death-throes. The New Testament's last words echo the longing of the whole Old Testament: 'Maranatha: Come Lord.'

But the New Testament is more than a prolongation of the Old. What makes its message unique is the claim that the Kingdom, while still remaining in some sense in the future, is in reality here, has in its essentials begun. The message on the lips of both John the Baptist and of Jesus is that the time has come, that the Kingdom of God is now upon us (see Mark 1:15). The miracles that fill the pages of the Gospels are seen as harbingers of the fact (see Matthew 11:2-6). Jesus is seen not simply as another prophet, but as the fulfilment of all that the prophets longed for. This is pressed home in both the preaching of the first disciples, and in the letters they wrote to the young churches they founded.

And the Gospels themselves have the same end in view. For they are not so much four biographies of Jesus as four proclamations of the Good News that in Jesus God's plans have reached their zenith, and heaven has come down to earth.

It is the Fourth Gospel which emphasises this message most insistently. Where the rest of the New Testament reflects something of the early Church's feeling that Jesus at his ascension had left his work unfinished, John stresses that God's plans were completed in Jesus, and that there is

nothing more to be added. For Jesus is the Word of God, the final revelation of all that God has to say about himself (John 1:1). Anyone who has seen Jesus has seen the Father (14:9), and there is nothing more to be seen. The Judgement of the world is not something still to come – it takes place here and now as people accept or refuse Jesus (3:19). Eternal life with God, so longed for by all people, is not something that lies in the future, beyond a resurrection from the dead – it is a reality present in the world through union with Jesus, who is the resurrection and the life (11:25). Jesus is not even to be thought of as having left the world – he continues to be with his disciples in a new and more effective way, through his holy Spirit (14:16-18). In short, the Kingdom is embodied in the very person of Jesus, who is the prototype of a new human relationship with God. Those who are united to him have already entered the fullness of the Kingdom.

Yet the Kingdom of God remains a paradox. Yes, it is achieved here and now in the Church's sharing of Jesus' death and resurrection. But it is also something for which the Church must continue to pray – 'Thy Kingdom come'. Yes, God's plans have come to their complete fulfilment, but except to the eyes of faith this remains hidden. In fact, in the eyes of the world, all goes on exactly as before. It is only in faith that Christians know that as followers of Jesus they have already been transported into heaven.

The life you have is hidden with Christ in God.
But when Christ is revealed
– and he is your life –
you, too, will be revealed with him in glory.
(Colossians 3:3-4)

Miracles

What is a miracle? For most people (witness the regular newspaper headlines) it is miracle enough that babies are born, or that friends have a surprising stroke of good luck, or that someone makes a remarkable recovery from sickness. All natural and earthbound events. They are hailed as 'miraculous' because each has an element of wonder, surprise, the unexpected, the new. And the religious person spontaneously sees in these utterly natural events the hand of the God of surprises.

Strangely, theologians have given the word a very different meaning, totally ethereal and otherworldly. For them, a miracle is not a miracle unless it contravenes the fixed and iron laws of nature. A miracle is the inexplicable, the 'impossible'. Water has to run uphill before it can be recognised as the handwriting of God.

This theology was based on a view of nature which only became popular in the 18th century, and has already been abandoned by most scientists. We live in a universe of surprises, and no scientist imagines there are no further surprises in the pipeline.

Neither does the Bible, which has no room for the idea

© Barnaby's Picture Library

of a 'fixed nature' occasionally violated by God. Everything about us is a marvel and a revelation. The very heavens are telling the glory of God. Each blade of grass speaks to the believer of the power of God. With this kind of world-view, the biblical authors could never have intended their miracle stories to be taken as evidence of God 'breaking into' our world: he had never been absent.

Since all religious traditions contain miracle stories, it is quite obvious that of themselves they prove nothing. Jesus himself is said to have rebuked those who came looking only for 'signs and wonders' (John 4:48). Paul even goes so far as to state that those who demand miracles simply show up their immaturity and lack of faith, and that those who come to 'belief' *because of* miracles are ultimately nothing less than unbelievers (see 1 Corinthians 14:20-22).

What then of the miracles attributed to Jesus in the Gospel pages? A number of points need to be made.

1. First, the tradition that Jesus was a healer is so constant, so widespread, and so uniform throughout the New Testament that only a fool would think it was fictitious. Remove those healing stories, and the Gospels simply fall to pieces. Nor do these stories create any particular difficulty. Healers there have always been, and they still thrive today. What they are able to achieve – for the blind, the deaf, the lame, the diseased, the mentally sick – may remain a mystery for most of us. But such healing tells us nothing about an intervening God: some healers have been self-confessed atheists. Jesus was quite certainly a healer, but to call his healing work 'miraculous' tells us, in itself, nothing.

2. An equally strong Gospel tradition indicates that Jesus had considerable reservations about his healing powers. The theme runs through the whole Gospel, from the opening story where he turns down the temptation to play the popular role of a wonder-working messiah, through the Peter story where he repudiates the idea of miraculously avoiding the cross as satanic, down to the Gethsemane story where he agonisingly turns his back on the same escape route. In the pages between, Jesus rebukes wonder-seekers

(John 6:26), describes miracle workers as possible deceivers (Matthew 7:23, 24:24), and calls those who demand signs from heaven 'an evil and unfaithful generation' (Matthew 16:4). There is an ambiguity about miracles which allows people to draw conclusions that are quite misleading.

3. And yet, wary as he was of the danger that they would be misinterpreted, Jesus was not slow to offer his own interpretation. For him, the many cures that accompanied his preaching were signs that God's Kingdom was being established in a godless world. Sickness and suffering, debility and disease, all of them the legacy of sin, were giving way to the healing power of a merciful God. The wounded human race was being restored to wholeness and health. 'If it is by the Spirit of God that I cast out demons, then the Kingdom of God has come upon you.' (Matthew 12:28 RSV) It was this meaning that Jesus invited people to grasp. They should not become mesmerised by the wonders themselves, which were no more than signposts or indicators. Someone who is pointing your gaze to the stars does not want you to continue staring at his finger.

4. It is the Fourth Gospel which puts most emphasis on the symbolic value of the miracle stories. For the author, each of the miracles he recounts is a 'sign', that is to say, a significant event, full of meaning. What the reader must look for, therefore, is not the nuts and bolts of the event ('How did he do it?'), but what it means. The event, however it may have registered on the Richter scale of history, points beyond itself to something far more important. And in each case, the 'beyond' that is being pointed to is the death of Jesus, where the glory of God will be manifested as never before. For the author, the cross is the wonder of all wonders, the ultimate revelation that God's power is the power of love.

5. Given this approach, the actual historical reality standing behind the Gospel miracle stories is now lost to us. It is impossible to reconstruct the original photographable event, simply because we only have access to it through the eyes

© Barnaby's Picture Library

of those who have already imposed their interpretation on it. Was the story of Cana originally a parable Jesus told, rather than an event in which he took part? Was the feeding of the multitudes originally only a token meal, of which the details later became exaggerated? Was the raising of the Galilean widow's son originally based on the story of 2 Kings 4, to show Jesus as even greater than Elisha? No one can answer such questions. Nor is it important, given the emphasis of the storytellers, that such questions should receive a definite yes or no. After all, which is more striking and worthwhile: incontrovertible evidence that Jesus actually did walk on water, or a story which expresses the faith of Jesus' disciples, that in him they experienced the invincible power of God?

The approach outlined above does not aim to get rid of the biblical miracles, but to understand them. It aims to restore a more biblical image of God, whose saving power is to be seen in what is natural, not in what is unnatural. It aims above all to reinstate Jesus of Nazareth as a human being, a man among men, not a Superman. Jesus was a man, and could do no more than any man fired by the Spirit of God can do. Yet in what he did, his disciples confessed that they had seen the glory of God present among them.

Jesus worked miracles. But since he was a human being they were the kind of miracles human beings can work. And so he presumed, quite naturally, that his disciples would work miracles greater than his own:

> *In all truth I tell you,*
> *whoever believes in me*
> *will perform the same works as I do myself,*
> *and will perform even greater works.*
>
> *(John 14:12)*

Scribes

In civilisations like our own, it is taken for granted that everyone can write. This is not true even today. It was certainly not true in older civilisations, where the ability to write was restricted to the privileged class of the educated, the 'scribes'.

The Israelite scribes, already honoured as scholars in their own right, came to special prominence in the Babylonian exile in the 6th century BC. With the destruction of palace and monarchy, temple and worship, independence and even nationality, Israel was forced back on to the only thing it had left, the Word of God in its sacred writings. It was the task of the scribes to assemble these writings, and preserve them for posterity by copying, editing and publishing them.

Most of the Old Testament began to take its present shape during this exile through the patient devotion of the scribes. It had become their vocation, as it were, to prepare Israel to recognise God's Word when it became embodied in the person of Jesus of Nazareth.

It was Jesus' complaint that they often failed in this

© Barnaby's Picture Library

vocation. Their familiarity with the Old Testament Law – they are frequently called 'lawyers' in the New Testament – had made them its interpreters, and sometimes its misinterpreters. Like the **Pharisees**, the party to which many of them belonged (see below), their temptation was to put more store by their human learning and traditions than by the Word of God entrusted to their care (Matthew 15:6). It was this which earned some of them the condemnation of Jesus (see Matthew 23), though there must have been many others who became his disciples (see Matthew 8:19, Mark 12:34).

Pharisees

The Pharisees have throughout history had a bad press. What they stood for has in many people's eyes become synonymous with formalism, casuistry, legalism, self-righteousness and hypocrisy.

This blanket judgement is unjust. It overlooks the fact that the whole purpose of the movement they instigated in the 2nd century BC was to 'separate' the people of God (that is the meaning of their name) from the pagan ways they were too readily adopting. Without their dedication and zeal to preserve the Old Testament ideal of a people apart, there would humanly speaking have been no one left to understand the message that Jesus was to preach.

As defenders of the living Word of God, which they insisted should be made available to all, they became by common consent the spiritual leaders of Judaism, at a time when the official priestly leadership had become almost entirely materialistic, and was soon to be obliterated. Their opposition to any kind of professional monopolisation of religion is well summed up in a saying of theirs: 'Better a learned bastard than an ignorant High Priest.'

In accepting this leadership, there was of course a danger of smugness and complacency. The meticulous observance of the Law could become an end in itself, and breed contempt for those who could not achieve such perfection. Some Pharisees fell into this danger, as some leaders of God's people have always done. Jesus did not hesitate to attack them in the same stinging terms as the prophets had used to call people to their senses (Matthew 23). But the danger was apparent to the Pharisees themselves, whose condemnation of their own complacent members was no less severe. It would be a mistake to make the whole of Pharisaism a scapegoat for the faults of the few.

Paul was a Pharisee, and was proud of it. So too were Nicodemus and Joseph of Arimathea, and no doubt many others who received the teaching of Jesus with open arms. If the Gospels seem too easily to identify the whole of the Pharisee party as Jesus' enemies, it should be realised that they were written at a time when positions had hardened, when Christianity had been forced to make a definitive break with a Judaism which still remained under Pharisee leadership. There is plenty of evidence that in historical fact the main conflict of the infant Church, as of Jesus, was with the priestly party of the *Sadducees* (see below), rather than with the Pharisees (see Acts 4:1, 5:17, etc).

When all this has been said, it still remains true that many of the Pharisees of Jesus' time tended to make the practice of religion centre upon self rather than upon God, and to make the Kingdom of God depend on human effort rather than on God's bounty. These strove to be perfect, but with the idea that this perfection could be presented to God as the price paid for salvation. It was this above all that brought them into collision with Jesus, whose message was that of all the prophets, that this was to make God into a slot-machine. It was to misunderstand the true nature of

© Barnaby's Picture Library

God, whose Kingdom is for all who admit their own nothingness and welcome his free gift.

It goes without saying that the attitude condemned by Jesus was not confined to the Pharisees. It was present within Christianity from the very beginning (see Acts 15:5), and continues at all times to threaten the Church's faithfulness to the spirit of the Gospel. Christians who listen to the parable of the Pharisee and the Publican and thank God that they are not like the Pharisee, are still far from the Kingdom.

Sadducees

The Sadducees seem to have taken their name from Zadok, the High Priest from whom the Jerusalem priesthood claimed to be descended. Together with other members of the Jewish upper classes, they formed an aristocracy which by New Testament times had succeeded in running the affairs of the nation, and their collaboration with the Greek and Roman occupying powers ensured that they maintained this prominent position. Their vested interest in the priesthood made them the sworn enemies of Pharisaism, which was largely a protest movement against Sadducee ritualism and monopolisation of religion.

Rigidly conservative and, unlike the Pharisees, opposed to any development of doctrine after the Babylonian exile, the Sadducees also found themselves as a body in conflict with Jesus, whose views on God's Kingdom differed so radically from theirs (see Luke 10:31), and whose attack on the temple system they never forgave (Mark 11:15-18). They played a leading part in bringing about Jesus' death (Mark 14:55), and were later prominent in a similar attempt to liquidate the infant Church (Acts 4:1, 5:17).

With the destruction of the temple in AD70, this priestly party disappeared from the pages of history, and the leadership of Judaism was taken over by their rivals, the Pharisees.

Resurrection

If Christ has not been raised, your faith is pointless and you have not, after all, been released from your sins.
(1 Corinthians 15:17)

The resurrection is often thought of as having no real bearing on our salvation. It was simply a divine mark of approval on the work which Jesus had already completed in his death, a kind of bonus stuck on afterwards. The quotation from Paul indicates how inadequate such a view is. To his mind, and to that of all the first preachers of the Gospel (see the sermons throughout Acts), the resurrection was the whole content of the Christian message, without which Jesus had not saved anyone, however many crucifixions he had undergone.

Why? For the Old Testament, death is not simply a temporary cessation of life. It is an annihilation, a collapse into the nothingness out of which the creator God first drew all things, and into which their own weight must draw them again should they ever claim independence of him. From such a death God had several times raised Israel as a nation, particularly from the graveyard of dry bones in exile (see Ezekiel 37). Could he also raise the individual from death?

For most of Old Testament history, the possibility was never considered. The descent into the underworld was the last journey people made, and they could look forward to nothing beyond (see Psalm 89:48, 115:17, etc). About 100BC, the book of Wisdom suggested that at death the soul went to God, even if the body was buried. But the Maccabean martyrs of the last century BC were not content with this solution. If God's promise to save his people was to be meaningful, then it must eventually include a resurrection of the whole person, body and soul, from the dead. How can one call people saved if only their soul has gone to heaven? Their body also longs for redemption (see Daniel 12:2, 2 Maccabees 7:9, etc).

The New Testament claims that this fullness of redemption was achieved in the person of Jesus of Nazareth. Totally identified with our situation of sinfulness and godlessness, he had accepted the final anguish of our exile from God in death. Yet that death was not the end of him. He did not die into nothing, but into God. By the power of God, he lives on as the Adam of an entirely new creation.

The New Testament announces this new creation as something that all people are destined to share. For the risen Christ is only the 'first-fruits of all who have fallen asleep' (1 Corinthians 15:20), and the rest of the harvest must follow before God's plans can be called complete. This will happen when 'he who raised Christ Jesus from the dead will give life to the mortal bodies' of those who live in the Spirit of Jesus (Romans 8:11). But this final glory is anticipated here and now in the Christian life, which is seen as a sharing in the new existence of the risen Jesus.

How are we to envisage this new existence of the Easter Jesus? It is not enough to say that the resurrection was *real*. The question is, what *sort* of reality was it? The sort of reality that could have been photographed, filmed and tape-recorded? The sort of reality that could have been witnessed by anyone present? By Pilate as well as by Peter? By Philip the tetrarch as well as by Philip the apostle?

There are many who would not only give an unhesitating Yes to these questions, but wonder why anyone would ask such silly questions. Of course the resurrection was visible, audible, tangible and measurable. Anything less objective and physical than that would not be a 'real' resurrection from the dead at all.

Others would find such an interpretation of the text too crude and materialistic. To believe that the resurrection was real, and not simply imaginary, does not require turning the risen Jesus into a resuscitated corpse. His meeting with his friends after his death was surely a reality at a far deeper level than mere eyes and ears can capture.

There are in fact plenty of indications in the text that the stories do not need to be taken as literally as they naïvely are taken by some readers. The brilliant stories of the empty tomb and of the appearances of the risen Jesus are not a diary of events. They are faith statements, dramatisations of the early Christian conviction that the Jesus who had been crucified lived on, and was now to be found not in the cemetery but among his disciples.

Can such a resurrection still be called 'bodily'? Only if bodiliness is seen as something that brings us close to each other, rather than as something that keeps us apart. If the risen Jesus really is closer to his friends now than he was in the days of his flesh, then he is more bodily than before, not less. His disciples now *are* his body, because he is embodied in them (see 1 Corinthians 12:27).

Messiah-Christ

The Hebrew word *messiah* translates into Greek as *christos*. Both words mean one who has been anointed. It was a title given to the Israelite kings, whose appointment was marked by the pouring of olive oil on their head, symbol of the strength given them by the holy Spirit of God (see 1 Samuel 10:1, 16:13, etc). Each of the kings of Israel therefore could be called a messiah or christ.

It was when one after another of the kings disappointed the high hopes that had been placed in them that the prophets began to turn their attention to the future king who, they hoped, would restore the golden age of their first king David, and complete the work which he had left unfinished (see Jeremiah 30:9, Ezekiel 34:23, Hosea 3:5, etc).

It was with this ideal king that the title 'Messiah' became more and more identified. Texts which had previously been composed in honour of David or his successors were applied to the new David of the future, in such a way that it is often no longer possible to distinguish between royal texts and specifically 'messianic' ones (for example, Psalms 2, 72, 110).

The New Testament writers seize on these texts and apply them without hesitation to Jesus, convinced that in him these Old Testament hopes had been realised. It was he who had come with that fullness of the Spirit that made him the Anointed One, the Messiah, the Christ for whom all these other anointings had been only preparations (see especially Acts 2:36). The promises of the Old Testament were now fulfilled in those who were 'anointed' with the Spirit that he poured out on them, whereby they became other 'Christs' or Christians.

Not everyone realises that this theme of a future king represents only one aspect of the Old Testament's 'messianic hope'. Both before the monarchy was instituted and after, there were those who expressed their hope of future salvation in terms of a new *Moses*, rather than of a new *David*. It was the ideal prophet, not the ideal king, who would speak the word of God to his people, and pour out upon them the Spirit with which he was filled, if necessary by his own suffering and death (see 'The Suffering Servant' on page 41 above).

There are even wilder dreams in some parts of the Old Testament. Disillusioned by the materialism and political ambition of their long line of kings, some Jews eventually rejected the hope of a royal Messiah, or indeed of any human saviour. God himself must be visibly reinstalled as king, and come into the midst of his people in as intimate a way as he had done in paradise (see Psalms 93-100, Isaiah 64:1, and the Wisdom literature). These examples of a 'Messianism without a Messiah' were just as genuine a part of Old Testament thought as the hopes expressed in terms of a human Messiah. And these too the New Testament takes up, to point to Jesus as their fulfilment.

Yet there is a recurrent Gospel theme which must also be mentioned: Jesus' reluctance to accept the title of Messiah. The theme is strongest in Mark. Even in the story of Peter's bold proclamation, Jesus issues a veto on using such a word about him (see Luke 9:21). In the trial before the High Priest and before Pilate, he answers the question about whether he claims to be Messiah with, 'You're using that word, not me.'

If this reluctance is based on fact, was Jesus reluctant to accept the title only because he repudiated the political overtones which the title had by then acquired? Or because he repudiated the title altogether? Whichever it was, the early Christians showed no such reluctance. They called him 'Jesus the Messiah-Christ' so readily that the word 'Christ' soon became no more than his surname. Their implication no doubt was that, whatever Jesus personally felt about the title, he is in fact the only Messiah this world will ever see. There is no other.

Son of God

The sons of God came to attend on Yahweh.
(Job 1:6)

Israel is my first-born son.
(Exodus 4:22)

I shall be a father to him (Solomon) and he a son to me.
(2 Samuel 7:14)

Blessed are the peacemakers:
they shall be recognised as children (sons) of God.
(Matthew 5:9)

Adam, son of God.
(Luke 3:38)

These quotations indicate how wide is the meaning of the title 'son of God'. The Bible uses it freely of anyone who in some way shares God's life, whether it be the angels who are the messengers sent out, as it were, from God's household, or the Israelite people among whom he had chosen to dwell, or the king who summed up the whole nation before God, or the just man who is the object of his special love, or indeed anyone who enjoys the gift of being God's creature.

The New Testament frequently uses the title of Jesus. In what sense? Certainly in nothing less than the senses mentioned above. The Good News it proclaims is precisely that the plan of God only imperfectly realised in the Old Testament has come to perfection in Jesus, who is the Messenger of God, the true Israel, the new David, the

perfectly just man, and the true brother of every Adam and Eve.

Not that this exhausts the meaning of the title as it is used in the New Testament. Although in some places it means no more than the awaited king-Messiah, in other places it suggests that God was Jesus' Father in a unique sense, and that his relationship with him was shared by no one else (see Matthew 11:27). This is emphasised especially in the Fourth Gospel, where the word son has, as it were, become Son with a capital S. Jesus is the *only* Son, who came forth from the bosom of the Father and must return there, whose activities are necessarily identified with the Father's, and who in the last analysis must say, 'The Father and I are one' (John 10:30) and, 'Anyone who has seen me has seen the Father' (John 14:9).

These are bold claims. They speak very clearly of the fact that in Jesus' life, as in no other life, his disciples had seen the truth of the proverb, 'Like father, like son'. They

© Barnaby's Picture Library

had seen that Jesus was a son who allowed God really to be his Father, and that in Jesus' life God proved he had a true son, that Jesus faithfully revealed the face of a Father who remains otherwise hidden, and that here was a true representative of God, able to stand in for God, and act on his behalf.

And yet, bold as the claims are, the title remains a metaphor. No one can literally be a 'son' of a God who has no wife. The metaphor emphasises the unique role that Jesus plays for his followers. But it was never meant to place him beyond their reach. Paul supposes throughout his letters that what Jesus became, every Christian is called to become. And the same John who writes so glowingly of Jesus as The Son, is not afraid to add:

You must see what great love the Father has lavished on us by letting us be called God's sons and daughters – which is what we are!
(1 John 3:1)

Beatitudes

The first discourse which Matthew puts on Jesus' lips opens with the 'Beatitudes' or Blessings. He is describing the candidates for the 'Kingdom of the Heavens' – a reverential Jewish paraphrase for the Kingdom of God. Who are the blessed, the really lucky ones? (Matthew 5:1-10)

The list does not – as is often imagined – promise eight different rewards for eight different virtues. All the eight mean the same thing. In fact, it is not a question of heavenly rewards at all, but of the qualifications required for bringing about God's Rule here and now. This Kingdom (or Promised Land, or Messianic Banquet, or Vision of God, or however one might describe it) does not go, as people might have expected, to the rich, the self-sufficient, those who have made a success of life. Paradoxically, it goes to the very opposite – to the poor and the unimportant, to the gentle and the sincere, to the hungry and the heartbroken.

This sort of people the world calls unfortunate. Jesus says they are the really fortunate ones, because nothing stands between them and God. In fact they are just like Jesus, who identified himself with such marginalised people, and in whom they were therefore able to see the face of God himself. How much more lucky can you get?

Infancy Gospels

The first two chapters of both Matthew and Luke are known as the Infancy Gospels. That these chapters are written in a different literary form from the rest of the Gospel material, and have therefore to be 'sung' in a quite different 'key', has long been recognised. They were clearly composed at a later stage than the Gospel that was first preached, which began not with Bethlehem but with the ministry of John the Baptist and the baptism of Jesus (see Acts 10:37 and the structure of the Gospels of Mark and John). They try to show the meaning of Jesus' life and ministry as if it had been foreshadowed in the events of his childhood.

They may therefore be compared to the Creation stories which occupy the first two chapters of the Old Testament, which set out to answer, not the question 'How?', but the question 'Why?'. In both cases, we are not reading a diary of past events, but listening in to a meditation on the meaning of things. In the case of Matthew and Luke, we are asked to see the meaning of Jesus in the light of a number of Old Testament themes.

Matthew has chosen four great themes: Moses and the Exodus, the Liberator-Judges, Kings and the Kingdom, and the Restoration from Exile. He has found a number of quotations which effectively evoke these themes – 'Out of Egypt . . .', 'Called a Nazarene . . .', 'Behold a Virgin . . .', 'From you Bethlehem . . .', 'A voice in Ramah . . .'. None of these texts are strictly speaking prophecies, in the sense of predictions of the future. But they are enough to show Jesus as much more than the remarkable second half of an equation. For Matthew he is the fulfilment not of a few texts, but of all that the Old Testament had been searching for, and the meaning behind all its questioning.

Luke's approach is even more artistic. He tells the story of the annunciation, nativity, circumcision, naming and infancy of Jesus, but only after he has told, (often in the same words) the story of the annunciation, nativity, circumcision, naming and infancy of John the Baptist. When it turns out that this story itself is told in the words of the infancy story of the opening chapters of 1 Samuel, Luke's purpose emerges. What he has devised is a triptych. One wing features Samuel the first of the prophets, and the other John the Baptist the last. In the centre panel stands Jesus, head and shoulders above both. Painted in the corners of this triptych are dozens of allusions to Old Testament texts (Gabriel, Elijah, God in Zion's midst, the Cloud covering the tabernacle, the Ark of the covenant, the Temple, the poor, the *Virgin* Israel (see below). The overall effect is to present Jesus, as Matthew does, as the answer to all the Old Testament's dearest dreams.

Such an understanding of the Infancy Gospels does not diminish them. To see them as rooted in Old Testament texts rather than as biography is not a loss, but an enrichment.

Virgin Birth

To speak of the people of God in the Old Testament as the 'Virgin Israel' is a metaphor. Yet it expresses eloquently the human barrenness, emptiness and poverty of a people who acknowledged themselves as totally dependent on the power of God to make them fruitful. Their salvation could not be of their own making, only an utterly gracious gift, a new creation which God alone could bring about.

The New Testament takes up this metaphorical language to apply it to Mary the mother of Jesus, whom it sees as the ideal towards which Israel had always been striving. It is only in the midst of such a humble and powerless Israel that God can become present among his people. Luke even quotes the prophet Zephaniah to present Mary as the embodiment of such a virginal Israel:

Rejoice . . . daughter of Jerusalem!	*Rejoice, so highly favoured!*
The Lord is king among you . . .	*The Lord is with you . . .*
Zion, have no fear,	*Mary do not be afraid;*
do not let your hands fall limp.	*you have won God's favour.*
The Lord your God is in your midst [womb]	*You are to conceive in the womb and bear a son*
a warrior who saves.	*and you must name him Jesus [the Lord saves].*
(Zephaniah 3:14-17)	*(Luke 1:28-31)*

Indeed, if the birth of any child can be greeted throughout the Old Testament as a gracious gift from God, how else speak of the Jesus who is seen as *the* Godsend of all time, the beginning of a new Israel? To speak of his birth from a virgin is to speak of the poverty and emptiness of a human race filled to overflowing by a God who is sheer grace.

To say that the Gospel language about Mary's virginity is a metaphor is to make no judgement about the biological circumstances of the birth of Jesus. The New Testament shows no interest in these. If they are thought to be relevant, they must be established on other grounds.

B. The Pauline Books

Unlike Mark and Matthew, Luke envisaged his Gospel as coming in two volumes. The first we have just considered. The second volume, now called Acts of the Apostles, forms a convenient bridge linking the Gospels with the Pauline Books which now follow. It introduces us to the gigantic figure of **Paul** (more about Paul on page 67), and gives us a background to his copious writings, which will eventually fill one third of the New Testament.

Acts of the Apostles

At first sight the book of Acts looks like a straightforward historical record of the first thirty years of the Church. It is not. Designed by Luke as the continuation of his Gospel, it is like his first volume a proclamation of faith. Its purpose is never merely historical but theological, to show that the Good News of what God did through Jesus became the Good News of what God continues to do through the Spirit of Jesus in the Church.

His story is therefore dominated by the **Spirit** (see page 66) of Jesus (the word occurs 57 times), and the events on which he concentrates are those which have a bearing on this message of salvation:
(a) the Pentecost event in which the early Church saw Jesus fulfilling his promise to return in order to be with his disciples for all time in his Spirit (chapters 1-5);
(b) the understanding of the universal implications of this event by such men as Stephen, Philip, Peter and Barnabas (chapters 6-12);
(c) the four great journeys in which Paul under the guidance of the Spirit took the Good News to the ends of the known world (chapters 13-28).
This brings to a satisfactory conclusion a story which in volume 1 had begun and ended in Jerusalem, but has acquired by the end of volume 2 a worldwide import.

> *You will be my witnesses not only in Jerusalem but throughout Judaea and Samaria, and indeed to earth's remotest ends.*
>
> *(Acts 1:8)*

Epistles

The word epistle means letter. The New Testament contains twenty-one of them, fourteen traditionally attributed to Paul. Their importance lies in the fact that they are among the earliest writings of the New Testament, and reveal how the meaning of Jesus' life was understood long before the first Gospel was written. At the same time, they were not composed in the abstract as set pieces of theology. They were clearly written impromptu and at dictation speed, to solve the problems and crises that arose in the early Christian communities. This occasionally makes them rather obscure, a fact recognised from the beginning (see 2 Peter 3:16). Even where they are clear, their full meaning does not really come across until we put them into the background against which they were written.

For this reason, the epistles of Paul are here dealt with in the order in which they were written, and not in the order in which they appear in our Bibles, which was established in the 4th century simply on the basis of their length and importance.

1 and 2 Thessalonians

The two letters to the northern Greek town of Salonika were written about AD50, soon after Paul's first mission there (Acts 17) had been cut short by persecution, and had left the little community doubtful about his continued interest in them. They were particularly concerned that the 'Second Coming' of Christ had not taken place as soon as they had been led to expect.

In the first letter, Paul reminds them of the enthusiasm with which they welcomed his preaching of the Gospel, and reassures them of his continued fatherly concern for them (chapters 1-3). He urges them to remain true to his teaching on purity and charity (chapter 4), and to keep their hopes focused on the Coming of Christ, when the salvation he has begun in them will be completed (chapter 5).

This letter apparently only worsened matters in Salonika. Many Christians concluded that the Coming of Christ was so close as to warrant giving up their jobs (2 Thessalonians 3:10-12). In a second letter, Paul has to assure them that many events, which Jesus promised would precede his Coming, had not yet come about (chapters 1-2). He urges them to peace and charity among themselves (chapter 3).

The two letters are remarkable for the light they throw on Paul's respect and tenderness towards his converts, and for the prominence they give to the glorious Coming of Christ, as the climax of his work of redeeming the living and the dead. On this, Paul will later need to revise his thoughts.

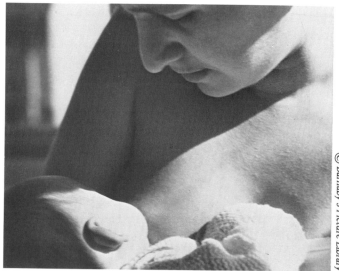

© Barnaby's Picture Library

Like a mother feeding and looking after her children, we felt so devoted to you, that we would have been happy
to share with you not only the gospel of God, but also our own lives, so dear had you become.
(1 Thessalonians 2:7-8)

1 and 2 Corinthians

While he was writing to Salonika, Paul was engaged in establishing a Christian community in pagan and licentious Corinth (Acts 18). From his headquarters in Ephesus between the years AD54 and 57, he conducted a considerable correspondence with his converts there, of which two letters survive. These are filled with concern lest his work in Corinth be ruined by later missionaries, whose over-intellectual approach to Christianity and lax moral standards had distorted the Gospel as Paul saw it, and split the Church into factions.

In the first surviving letter, Paul's aim is primarily to ensure the Corinthian Church's loyalty to himself. He castigates the worldly-wise approach which is rending the Body of Christ (chapters 1-4), and desecrating it by a to pagan standards of morality (chapters 5-6). He dresses at greater length the problems on which his converts had written to ask his advice: about celibacy (chapter 7), about eating food left an liturgies (chapters 8-10), about the gy (chapter 11), about the attitude to be taken (chapters 12-14) (more about charisms on bout the Christian belief in the resurrection pter 15). He finishes the letter with an for the poor Christians in Jerusalem

seems to have had the effect Paul hoped for. 2 Corinthians a little later, the abuses been corrected, and he could freely express e reaffirmation of his authority (chapters 1-7), tack the critics who had tried to undermine it 13). In the intervening chapters 8-9, he again ntributions to his Jerusalem Relief Fund, which as a concrete expression of his good relationship the mother Church of Jerusalem.

The two letters are the most personal of Paul's correspondence and more than any other reveal his dynamic personality, on fire with love for Christ, and for his converts. They contain two of the finest passages in the New Testament, the famous rhapsody on charity in 1 Corinthians 13 ('a portrait for which Jesus sat', someone has called it), and his embarrassed record of his own achievements in 2 Corinthians 11-12.

I am glad of weaknesses, insults, constraints,
persecutions and distress for Christ's sake.
For it is when I am weak that I am strong.
(2 Corinthians 12:10)

Philippians

Philippi is the first European town anyone would reach coming from the east. Paul preached the Gospel there about AD50, shortly before reaching Salonika (Acts 16).

Five years later, headquartered in Ephesus on his third journey, he was near enough to hear frequently from his converts there. About the same time that he was conducting his lengthy correspondence with Corinth therefore, he wrote a short letter to the Philippians as well, warning them

of the same rival missionaries who he felt were distorting the Christian message (chapter 3).

The rest of the letter is a miscellany of news, thanks for the presents sent to him, and fatherly advice on mutual charity. It is typical of Paul that, in searching for an example to illustrate this last topic, he should have given us the New Testament's most priceless statement on Jesus' self-sacrifice:

You must face life as Jesus did:

Like Adam, he was the image of God;
but unlike Adam, did not presume
that being like God meant to domineer.

He knew it meant to renounce all claims,
except the claim to be servant of all.

So he lived the life of a man among men,
and accepted the lot of men, which is death,
even the shameful death of a slave.

That is why God has raised him up,
and bestowed a title beyond compare:

Every creature, living and dead,
will kneel to him, and give glory to God,
and echo the cry, 'Jesus is Lord'.
(Philippians 2:5-11, author's translation)

© Barnaby's Picture Library

Galatians

About the same year AD57, either while he was still in Ephesus or had moved on to Corinth in his third missionary journey, Paul wrote to the Christians of Galatia. The term seems to refer to the Asia Minor churches he had founded in his very first journey in Pisidian Antioch, Iconium, Derbe and Lystra (Acts 13), and had revisited on later journeys (Acts 16 and 19).

It was in these churches that the rival Jewish-Christian missionaries, only hinted at in Corinthians and Philippians, were most active. And it is in this letter that Paul makes his strongest attack on them, to repudiate once for all their view of Christianity which would make salvation something that people could earn by their own self-sufficient 'works' or efforts.

He angrily defends his own presentation of the Gospel as the only genuine one, the one preached by the other apostles (chapters 1-2). He insists that our right standing before God ('justification') is a free gift, given by God through Christ to a world that can do nothing but abandon itself to such a gift by faith (chapters 3-4). He pleads that this newly-won freedom of the full-grown children of God, indwelt by the very Spirit of Jesus, should not be thrown away in favour of a juvenile system of 'keeping the law' (chapters 5-6).

© Eastern Counties Newspapers

The letter inevitably contains some obscure passages. But it also concludes with the magnificent statement in which Paul sums up his Gospel.

> *It is out of the question that I should boast at all,*
> *except of the cross of our Lord Jesus Christ,*
> *through whom the world has been crucified to me,*
> *and I to the world.*
>
> *(Galatians 6:14)*

Romans

The epistle to the Christians of Rome is a fuller and calmer exposition of the subject dealt with in Galatians. It was written soon afterwards from Corinth, where Paul had finally settled the Corinthian crisis, and was preparing to return to Palestine to conclude his third missionary journey before starting on a fourth to Rome and Spain (Acts 19-20).

The Roman Church had already been founded by other missionaries, including perhaps Peter himself. But since Rome would be the natural headquarters of the evangelisation which Paul was planning further westwards, he wished to present the Christians there with a full statement of the meaning of the Gospel as he saw it in the year AD57. It is the nearest attempt Paul ever made to analyse his faith systematically, and for that reason will always have pride of place among his epistles.

He presents the Gospel in the following terms. Where the law of nature and the Law of Moses have both failed to restore man's friendship with God, God himself has stepped in, and in Christ reconciled to himself all those willing to commit themselves to Christ by faith (chapters 1-8). In doing this, God has not gone back on his Old Testament promises, but fulfilled them: the new Israel has been grafted on to the old (chapters 9-11). In the light of this, Paul urges both Gentile and Jewish Christians to show respect and consideration for each other, and so reflect in their dealings with each other God's own love for them (chapters 12-16).

> *I am certain of this:*
> *neither death nor life, nor angels, nor principalities,*
> *nothing already in existence and nothing still to come . . .*
> *will be able to come between us and the love of God*
> *known to us in Christ Jesus our Lord.*
>
> *(Romans 8*

Colossians

Paul reached Rome as he had hoped, but in
20-28). From his Roman prison during the ye
he wrote to the Asian towns he had evange
Ephesus during his third journey. Of these,
one of the most important.

He had heard rumours that his conve
being infected with a curious Asian 'myste!
which thought of God as completely unatta
worshipped the angels instead. Of these sup
intermediaries, Christ was merely the highes

To counteract this unorthodox form of C
Paul presents the true 'mystery' of Christian be
Godhead, far from being beyond our reach, exists
fullness in the man Jesus. God has himself spanned
immeasurable distance between heaven and earth, in Ch
(chapters 1-2). This mystery is continued in the Christia
who, united to Christ, already lives as it were in heaven
(chapters 3-4).

> *God wanted all fullness to be found in him*
> *and through him to reconcile all things to him,*
> *everything in heaven and everything on earth.*
>
> *(Colossians 1:19-20)*

ΠΑΥΛΟΣ
ΦΙΛΗΜΟΝΙ
ΕΝ ΚΟΛΟΣΣΑΙΣ

In the postbag along with the letter to Colossae, Paul enclosed a short note to one of its outstanding church members, whose runaway slave Paul had converted in

Rome. It is a moving appeal to Philemon to pardon this slave, whom he has the legal right to kill but who is now his brother in Christ. The courtesy and delicacy of this letter makes it one of the most precious pages in the New Testament.

> *If he has wronged you in any way,*
> *put it down to my account.*
>
> *(Philemon 18)*

Ephesians

As Romans was a fuller and calmer statement of Galatians, so Ephesians is a fair copy of Colossians. With no further [ne]ed to deal with personalities (the letter was probably a [circu]lar, addressed to all the Churches governed from [Ephesus]), and with no more controversy to distract him, [he is fin]ally able to present an orderly and balanced [survey. If] the epistle really is Paul's own (some scholars [attrib]ute it to a later disciple), then this is his final [look at th]e Gospel, as it has matured in his mind by the [end of his life.]

[In the las]t analysis, God's plans are seen to be fulfilled [through] the Church which is as it were an [incarnation of Ch]rist through history (chapters 1-3). This [oneness of Christia]ns in the Body of Christ is incompatible [particu]larly with the sin of uncharity, for their [love of each] other is the measure of their attitude to the [Christ with whom] they are one (chapters 4-6).

> *[Living] by the truth and in love,*
> *[we shal]l grow completely into Christ,*
> *[who is t]he head by whom the whole Body is joined*
> *together.*
>
> *(Ephesians 4:16)*

[1] and 2 Timothy

More serious doubts have been expressed about Paul's part in writing the letters to Timothy and Titus. The last chapters of Acts give the impression that he was executed immediately after his Roman imprisonment, in AD63, and these epistles cannot be dated earlier than 65. But it is possible that Paul was released from the imprisonment described in Acts, and was able to return to the east before being sent to Rome a second time, and that he was not executed until the year AD67. In that case, the three letters would have been written shortly before and during his second imprisonment, as a last anxious appeal to his successors to safeguard the 'deposit', the body of truth he has handed on to them. The author of these letters tends to be a back-seat driver.

Timothy was a convert of Paul's (Acts 16:1) and one of his most constant companions on his missionary journeys. The first epistle presumes he is now in Ephesus as overseer of the Asian Churches, and that he is meeting there the same unorthodox Christianity that Paul was fighting earlier in Colossae. Writing from Greece, Paul warns him against this travesty, and urges him to remain loyal to the apostolic teaching he has received, and to hand it on to worthy and

© Barnaby's Picture Library

carefully chosen successors. The Church is passing from the enthusiasm of its youth into a more organised custodian of the truth.

The second letter repeats these warnings even more movingly from the Roman prison where Paul knows that his martyrdom is near, and where in his loneliness he hopes that Timothy will be able to see him again before the end.

> *I have fought the good fight to the end;*
> *I have run the race to the finish;*
> *I have kept the faith . . .*
> *Make every effort to come and see me*
> *as soon as you can.*
>
> *(2 Timothy 4:7-9)*

Titus

This short letter is almost entirely parallel to 1 Timothy, and repeats its advice for the benefit of Titus, another of Paul's travelling companions, now overseer of the Church in Crete. It contains some fine and succinct expressions of the Christian faith.

> *The kindness and love of God our Saviour for mankind*
> *have been revealed.*
>
> *(Titus 3:4)*

Hebrews

The doubts which have been raised over Paul's connection with the epistles at the tail-end of the Pauline collection, have been solved in reference to Hebrews. It is certain that Paul did not write it. This can be gathered not only from its style and its lack of Paul's signature, but also from the early tradition which placed the epistle, in spite of its importance and length, at the very end of the Pauline writings.

It was perhaps written by one of Paul's disciples soon after Paul had died, when the Roman War against the Jews (AD67-70) was tempting a group of recently converted 'Hebrews' to go back to the faith of their fathers and die fighting with their own people. It urges them to look again at their Old Testament, and realise more deeply that the Gospel does not contradict it, but fulfils it.

All its themes lead to Jesus. He is God's last Word, revealing all there is to know about him (chapters 1-2). He is the new Moses leading the human race to the true Jerusalem (chapters 3-4). He is the new High **Priest** (more about Priest on page 68) opening up the sanctuary of heaven (chapters 5-7). He is the new Sacrifice reconciling people to God (chapters 8-9).

In the light of these themes, the letter pleads with its readers not to be swayed by their feelings of human loyalty, but to hang on to Jesus with a faith like Jesus' own (chapters 10-13).

Let us keep our eyes fixed on Jesus,
who leads us in our faith and brings it to perfection.
(Hebrews 12:2)

Things to do . . .

Paul's epistles have been compared to listening in to one end of a telephone conversation. Take one of the letters he wrote to Corinth, and try to reconstruct the other end of the conversation. What were the Corinthians telling and asking Paul?

Paul has paid a visit to your parish. As a group, compose the epistle he later sent to you.

Read through one of Paul's epistles and make a list of your favourite quotations. Compare the lists composed by your group.

Holy Spirit

Many people find the idea of the Holy Spirit highly confusing, especially when it is expressed in the old English form of the 'Holy Ghost'. Even the term, 'The Third Person of the Blessed Trinity' is of little comfort to them, and can confuse some people even more. Perhaps they would find the biblical development of the word more helpful.

Spirit, in both Hebrew and Greek, means 'breath'. When it is metaphorically applied to God – the 'Spirit of God' – it refers to his creative power. The Bible supposes that the world was first brought into being by this Spirit of God (Genesis 1:2), and is peopled by those into whom God had breathed his Spirit (Genesis 2:7). The great leaders of Israel – Moses, Joshua, David, Mary – are said to be insp[ired] and empowered by this Spirit of God, and the prophe[ts are] those who are so open to God's 'breath' that what c[omes] out of their mouth is the very word of God. The O[ld] Testament yearns for the day when everyone, y[oung and] old, men and women, will be invigorated by th[is] Spirit (Joel 3:1).

The New Testament presents Jesus as th[e one in] whom that hope begins to be realised. On hi[m the Spirit] not only comes down as on his ancestors, bu[t in a] permanent way (John 1:33). His whole life i[s under the] guidance of that Spirit of love and holiness w[hich is] at one with God, and his ministry is marked [by an] authority, a sensitivity and openness, which [people] acknowledge to be of God. Himself full of the [Spirit] (Luke 4:1), his burning wish is to share this c[lose] relationship with God with the rest of his broth[ers and] sisters, whatever the cost (Luke 12:49).

In the event, the cost is Calvary. It is there t[hat Jesus] shows the extent of the self-giving that is entailed in [true] godliness. That is why John's Gospel point to the cros[s (John] 19:30) as the moment when Jesus bequeathes his own [deeply] godly Spirit on all his disciples. They will be as close to Go[d] as he was, and know God as intimately as he knew him, as soon as they begin to live as he did (John 15:26).

The early Church therefore easily speaks of God's Holy Spirit as the Spirit of Jesus: it was through the death of Jesus that the first Christians first fully experienced this mysterious reality. Nor do they think of this Spirit, palpably present in their midst, as a poor substitute compensating for the absence of Jesus. On the contrary, they are aware that in the Spirit Jesus is forever present with his friends, and more wonderfully than in the days of his flesh (John 14:17-18). The 'fellowship of the Holy Spirit' is precisely the fulfilment of Jesus' promise never to desert his followers (John 14:3).

The reality of all this cannot be proved to non-believers. According to John, Jesus said that it could only be measured by the godliness and Christ-likeness of Christians, that is to say, by the love they show for each other (John 13:35).

Paul

The life of Paul is easily told. He was born at Tarsus, a university city on the coast of Asia Minor, at about the same time as Jesus. The son of devout Pharisee parents, he grew up with a zeal for the Jewish religion which he later boasted none of his contemporaries could match. Though he studied in Jerusalem he never met Jesus in the flesh, but this was more than compensated for by his meeting with the risen Christ on the Damascus road, at a moment when he was hell-bent on exterminating the flourishing group of Christians who seemed, to his alert mind, to be undermining the Judaism he held so dear. The meeting turned his life inside out. He became a Christian, and spent the next ten years meditating on the unexpected fulfilment [of] Judaism in the Gospel. But these were only years of [prepar]ation for the amazing career that was to follow. [When] Barnabas called him out of retirement, he was [to se]t the world on fire. Within a dozen years he had [nea]rly 8,000 miles in three vast missionary [... bro]adcasting the Christian Good News to people [... the o]utward looking Church was as yet scarcely [... build]ing up thriving centres of Christianity in [... Asia M]inor, Macedonia and Greece. He had even [... a fourt]h journey to Rome, but he reached it in [... the victi]m of the hatred of his fellow-Jews, who [... regarded] him as a traitor to their cause. He was [... on a c]harge of treason against Rome in the year [... outside th]e city on the road to Ostia, where his tomb [... bears] the simple inscription: 'Paul, Apostle and [Martyr'.]

[Paul's char]acter is less easy to summarise. His copious [correspondence] fills a third of the New Testament, and [is an eloqu]ent witness to the complex mass of [contradic]tions he must have been. Inflexible and even harsh [with any]one who questions his authority, he yet disarms his [reader]s throughout by his genuine tenderness and humility. [Ag]ain and again he finds himself incapable of resisting the [te]mptation to enter the most profound theological argument, yet it invariably ends with an application that is utterly practical. A tornado of enthusiasm and energy, hardly pausing for breath either in his missionary work or in his dictated letters, he nevertheless treats his converts with a courtesy and delicacy which won all hearts. It is not surprising that he was deeply loved not only by all who met him in his travels, from the housewives in Corinth to the Ephesus dockers, but also by all who throughout history have made the effort to meet him in his epistles. St Catherine of Siena called him *Quel Paoluccio*, 'That darling Paul'.

Yet Paul's true greatness does not lie merely in his attractive character. It lies in the vital part he played in the formation of the infant Church. Called at a time when Christianity could have remained a sect within Judaism, it was he who saw more clearly than anyone its world-wide potential and mission. This insight was his from the moment of his conversion, when it was borne upon him that the Jesus whose memory he was trying to efface was not a dead figurehead of the past, but one who through his resurrection had entered the very glory of God, and who therefore lived on through his Spirit in the Church.

PAUL'S MISSIONARY JOURNEYS
"Continually travelling" (2 Corinthians 11:26)

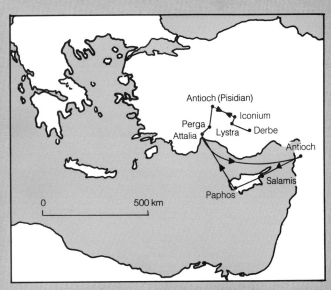

1st Journey (Acts 13-14)

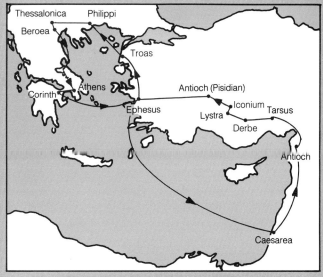

2nd Journey (Acts 16-18)

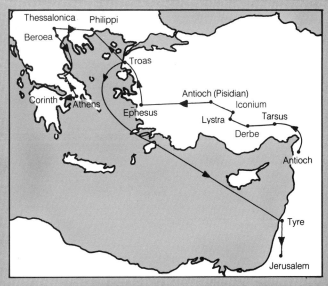

3rd Journey (Acts 19-21)

67

Christianity, Paul saw, cannot be envisaged as a system of rules and regulations to tie people down to the practices they have undertaken, but a new life lived in the risen Christ, in whom God has brought all creation and history to its climax, and in whom the Christian has already been caught up into the presence of the Father. In this final consummation of God's plan for the human race, all human barriers have been broken down.

> *There can be neither Jew nor Greek,*
> *there can be neither slave nor freeman,*
> *there can be neither male nor female –*
> *for you are all one in Christ Jesus.*
>
> (Galatians 3:28)

Priest

The New Testament interprets the role of Jesus by means of many different metaphors – Son, Word, Servant, Shepherd, etc. 'Priest' is one of the strangest, given the fact that he was unmistakably a layman, and the very antithesis of everything the word 'priest' stood for in New Testament times.

Priests had ruled the nation ever since the monarchy had perished in Babylonian exile. Their ideals had once been high – to turn the Jewish people into a priestly community, whose only raison d'être was to make the whole of their life a worship of God. But centuries of ritualism and professionalism had taken their toll. By New Testament times the priesthood had become an empty shell, and the real religious leadership of the nation had been lost to the lay opposition movement of the Pharisees. Jesus' opposition to the 'religion' of the priests was no less absolute. Their response was to engineer his death.

In spite of such a violent confrontation, the New Testament writers were not slow to realise that the old priestly ideals had found a new expression in the lay life of Jesus, and eagerly took up the language of priesthood, though not the word 'priest' (except in Hebrews), to apply it to him. They saw him as the supreme mediator between God and the human race (1 Timothy 2:5), and his life as a work that made God and the world 'at-one' (2 Corinthians 5:19). They saw his death as a sacrifice offered to God (Romans 3:25), and his risen body as a new temple (John 2:21) enshrining the very presence of God on earth. They saw his followers, therefore, as constituting a new priesthood (1 Peter 2:5), no longer by profession or ordination, but simply by being incorporated into that Body. Such priests are called to make their whole lives an act of worship (Romans 12:1), not by ritual, but by living as Jesus did.

Charisms

Charism is a Greek word meaning 'gift'. It is [used] in the New Testament as a technical term for [the] gifts that were thought to have been conferred [on the] Church by the Christ who lived on among his [people in the] Spirit.

Paul gives several lists of these charisms. He [includes] among them not only the 'extraordinary' gifts of he[aling,] ecstasy, miraculous power, etc., but also the quite ['ordinary'] gifts of preaching, teaching, social service, even marria[ge] (1 Corinthians 7:7). In short, for Paul, all Christians, ins[ofar] as they have a role to play in the Church, whether it is spectacular or insignificant, receive the precise charism they need to do so (see Ephesians 4:7-13).

When some of his converts at Corinth were boasting about the spectacular charisms they thought had been bestowed on them, Paul reminded them that in a body the insignificant functions are often more vital than the ostentatious ones. And the Church, says Paul, is a Body, in which every Christian has been incorporated into Christ, and where the most important charism is charity, without which the whole Body will disintegrate (see 1 Corinthians 12-14).

68

C. The General Epistles

Alongside the letters associated with the name of Paul, the first Christians were anxious to preserve a number of letters written by other early Church leaders. Not being addressed, as Paul's were, to specific communities but to the Church in general, they are sometimes known as the catholic or universal epistles.

James

The epistle of James is probably one of the earliest writings of the New Testament. Written about AD50, it claims to be [the] work of the James who was head of the Christian [comm]unity in Jerusalem, a relative of Jesus (see Acts 15). [It is] addressed in general to all Christian converts from [u]nder pressure from the society in which they [conf]orm to wordly standards. James urges them to [live] the spirit of the Sermon on the Mount (of [which the]re many echoes), in the conviction that it is [the hu]mble and the persecuted that are God's

[His] approach to the relationship of Christian [faith w]ill later give problems to Paul, who [sees the q]uestion in a significantly different way. So [for w]hom this was 'a right strawy epistle'.

[T]his faith of yours without deeds!
[...] deeds that I will show you my faith.

(James 2:18)

[Pet]er

[1 Pet]er is addressed to the Christians of Asia Minor, [suffer]ing like James' addressees from the hostility of the [worl]d in which they lived. It has generally been accepted as [th]e work of the apostle Peter, writing during his last years in Rome, probably about AD65.

Peter consoles his correspondents by reminding them of their baptism, when they accepted Jesus' death as their own in order to share in the glory of his resurrection, and when like Jesus they agreed to turn their back on worldly standards in order to set out on the journey that would lead

them to God's Kingdom. This does not remove them from the stern reality of everyday life, but it does mean that in their various relationships with the world, they must always show their homesickness for heaven.

The epistle has so many references to baptism, the exodus journey and the resurrection, that it has been plausibly argued that it was originally a sermon for use in the baptismal liturgy (preached by Peter himself?), eventually adapted into a letter to be shared by all.

Blessed be God the Father of our Lord Jesus Christ,
who in his great mercy has given us a new birth into a
living hope
through the resurrection of Jesus Christ from the dead.

(1 Peter 1:3)

Jude

This short letter was written about the year AD80, apparently by the brother of James. It is directed against the kind of philosophical speculation with which Paul had to deal in Colossae (see page 64 above), and which threatened to reduce Christ to a sort of superior angel. Jude fiercely condemns this unorthodox form of Christianity, and urges his Asia Minor readers to remain true to the teaching of the apostles.

I felt that I must write to you
encouraging you to fight hard for the faith
which has been once and for all entrusted to God's
holy people.

(Jude 3)

2 Peter

The letter known as 2 Peter has incorporated the whole of Jude's letter as its second chapter, and added to it an assurance that the Coming of Christ will finally destroy the notion that heaven and earth cannot meet (chapters 1 and 3).

The epistle was written towards the end of the first century, when Paul's letters were already accepted as 'Scripture' (3:16), and Peter was already long dead. His name is used by the author in rather the same way as the name of Isaiah is used by the later contributors to his book, out of a sincere conviction that this addition to his work is a genuine interpretation and development of it in new circumstances.

I shall take great care that after my own departure
you will still have a means to recall these things to mind.

(2 Peter 1:15)

Things to do . . .

Taking 1 Peter 1:3 – 5:11, make a list of all the direct and indirect references to Christian baptism.

Compare what Paul says about Abraham's faith in Galatians 2:15 – 3:22 with what is said in James 2:14 – 3:22. How deep do the differences go?

D. The Johannine Books

The final group of New Testament books comprises those that were probably the last to be written. They are all associated with the name of John. Four of them (the epistles and the Gospel) are clearly from the same hand, and the fifth has a considerable number of links with the ideas expressed there. The extent to which they are the work of John the apostle is disputed, but the tradition attributing the epistles and the Gospel to him is so strong that it can be assumed that at least John's memoirs ultimately stand behind these writings.

John's Gospel

In its present form, the Fourth Gospel was written considerably later than the others, say about AD95, and is the most profound of the four. Its language is simplicity itself, but beneath it lies the most searching reflection on the mystery of Christ. John has been called 'The Theologian'. This makes him easier to read than the others, because he makes quite explicit what the others leave implicit, that we are not dealing with a biography of Jesus but with an interpretation in retrospect of the meaning of his life and work.

For John, Jesus is the Word of God, in whom God has told the world all that he can say of himself. Each event in Jesus' life spells out this truth to those who have ears to hear. The miracle stories in particular are not to be seen simply as so many displays of power, but as 'signs', all of them pointing to this one reality.

© Barnaby's Picture Library

To serve this symbolic purpose, John has been most careful in his choice of the stories he tells, usually the ones neglected by the other evangelists. He presents Jesus as the Life of God, finally made available to the human race, and illustrates this in the stories of Nicodemus, the cripple, the Samaritan woman, and the desert meal (chapters 3-7). Jesus is likewise the Light that God has shone in the darkness to overcome it, and this is seen in the stories of the blind man,

the good Shepherd, the disputes with the Pharisees, and the raising of Lazarus (chapters 8-11). Jesus is the very Glory of God, in whom God has come to dwell on earth, as the stories of Bethany, Palm Sunday, and the Last Supper illustrate (chapters 12-17).

This divine Glory is finally made most manifest in Jesus' passion, death and resurrection (chapters 18-20), where Jesus shows most clearly what God truly is – not a policeman but a lover. Believers are invited to enter that glory of God, not in another world, but here and now, in their own self-sacrifice and love. John's most distinctive contribution to the New Testament is his insistence that the 'eschatological realities' – coming of Christ, resurrection, judgement, eternal life – are not tomorrow, but today.

1, 2 and 3 John

No one doubts that these three letters came from hand as the Fourth Gospel, and so the question the authorship of the Gospel are inevitably refl In the epistles he calls himself the 'Elder'. If t John the apostle, then it must be presumed t end of his life (AD90-100) he was a sort of pa Ephesus, in charge of all the churches in Asi

The three letters are all concerned wi philosophy which formed the background New Testament epistles (Colossians, Ephes Titus, Jude, 2 Peter), according to which the was thought to be attainable only by some s intellectual insight which had nothing to do behaviour of the body, and Jesus was regarde half-god who brought this insight to the world to this unorthodox Christian philosophy by stre apostolic tradition on the uniqueness of Christ, a underlining the uselessness of a faith that does not into holiness of life.

3 John seems to have been the first to be written. a short note congratulating a prominent Church member, Gaius, for standing out against the seductive philosophy. Ye the curious heresy seems to have spread, and 2 John was written to another Christian community (here called 'The Chosen Lady') to warn them of its dangers.

1 John finally sets out the fullness of the traditional Christian teaching on the matter – that God is love, that this love has become incarnate in the person of Jesus Christ, and that Christians, united to God in Christ, must express their faith by a holiness and a love for others which reflect God's own holiness and love. This has expressed in abstract form the meaning that lies at the heart of the stories in the Fourth Gospel.